Proverbs and Their Lessons

Richard Chenevix Trench

Edited by

Wolfgang Mieder

"Proverbium"
in cooperation with the
Department of German and Russian

The University of Vermont
Burlington, Vermont
2003

Supplement Series

of

Proverbium
Yearbook of International Proverb Scholarship

Edited by Wolfgang Mieder

Volume 13

Cover illustration taken from:
John Bromley, *The Man of Ten Talents: A Portrait of Richard
Chenevix Trench 1807-86. Philologist, Poet, Theologian, Archbishop.*
London: S.P.C.K., 1959.

ISBN 0-9710223-4-8

Manufactured in the United States of America
by Queen City Printers Inc.
Burlington, Vermont

INTRODUCTION

As scholars, we all stand on the shoulders of giants, and it behooves us to acknowledge our debts to these precursors. This allusion to a classical proverb also holds true for paremiographers and paremiologists. There is no doubt that both F. Edward Hulme in his still valuable study of *Proverb Lore* (London: Elliot Stock, 1902; rpt. Detroit: Gale Research Company, 1969) and Archer Taylor in his magisterial and unsurpassed treatise on *The Proverb* (Cambridge, Mass.: Harvard University Press, 1931; rpt. Hatboro, Penn.: Folklore Associates, 1962; rpt. again with an introduction by Wolfgang Mieder. Bern: Peter Lang, 1985) benefitted greatly from a small volume on proverbs which, somewhat surprisingly, they each mention but once in passing (p. 64 and p. 144, respectively). Both scholars are greatly indebted to this volume, which contains scholarly and ethical elements that are of considerable value still today.

This only apparently mysterious book was originally published in 1853 by Richard Chenevix Trench with the title of *On the Lessons in Proverbs* and consisted of six lectures that he had presented to Young Man's Societies around Portsmouth, England. The volume went through seven editions during Trench's lifetime and several more later on, including a final edition with additional notes and a bibliography prepared by A. Smythe Palmer in 1905 with the slightly changed title *Proverbs and Their Lessons* for the well-known

London publishing firm of George Routledge. The publication history of this slim volume of less than two-hundred pages is ample proof that it was an important and influential survey on the origin, nature, distribution, meaning, and significance of proverbs in the English-speaking world.

Its author Richard Chenevix Trench (1807-1886) was a major figure in literary and church circles of Great Britain, as can best be seen from John Bromley's biographical study *The Man of Ten Talents: A Portrait of Richard Chenevix Trench 1807-86. Philologist, Poet, Theologian, Archbishop* (London: S.P.C.K., 1959). He was educated at Trinity College, Cambridge, and as an Anglican clergyman became dean of Westminster and archbishop of Dublin. He was an incredibly prolific author, publishing his own poetry, anthologies, translations, and works dealing with history, the church, and philology. Many of his books appeared in numerous editions and have been reprinted in Great Britain and the United States. Among his philological books are *On the Study of Words* (1851), *English Past and Present* (1855), and *A Select Glossary of English Words* (1859). His paper *On Some Deficiencies in Our English Dictionaries* (1857) was instrumental in commencing the work on the Oxford *New English Dictionary*. Clearly philological issues occupied Trench's mind during the 1850s, and this work, together with his interest in ethics and religion, led him quite naturally to the study of proverbs as well.

As already mentioned, his volume on *Proverbs and Their Lessons* is composed of six lectures whose titles clearly reveal its major thrust and content. While the book is meant to be a contribution to the language, nature, content, and function of proverbs, it is also designed to preach a bit of common-sense wisdom about life in general and religious morality in particular. Lecture I on "The Form and Definition of a Proverb" discusses the common sense, knowledge, and human nature expressed in proverbs while at the same time citing various definitions and examples taken from collections and literature in numerous languages. Lecture II on "The Generation of Proverbs" looks at the Greek and Latin proverb tradition, proverbs of the Bible, and medieval Latin proverbs. Many of these texts were translated into the vulgate languages, resulting in a common stock of proverbs in Europe and beyond. But Trench also shows how "new" proverbs based on events, names, and regional concerns are created to add to the international stock of proverbs. Lecture III on "The Proverbs of Different Nations Compared" reveals Trench's cross-cultural and inter-disciplinary methodology. He warns against the danger of looking for national character traits in proverbs, stressing instead that many proverbs express universal concerns of humanity. He presents many Greek, Latin, Spanish, Italian, German and English proverbs, always pointing out similarities and differences.

Lecture IV on "The Poetry, Wit and Wisdom of Proverbs" deals with the imagery, the poetic expression, and the sapiential message of proverbs. While proverbs contain shrewd common sense, they actually come alive only in actual speech contexts where they serve various functions. Lecture V on "The Morality of Proverbs" juxtaposes coarse and immoral proverbs with those that exhibit and teach ethical values. Trench cites many unworthy, base, profane, and evil proverbs, but he indicates that there are also those worthy, noble, religious, and basically good proverbs that serve as commonly accepted laws of life and civil conduct. Lecture VI represents a natural continuation of this analysis by dealing with "The Theology of Proverbs," a matter close to Trench's heart as a clergyman. Proverbs are seen as weapons against such evil forces as the devil; they are very useful pieces of wisdom for sermons; and at their best proverbs contain moral messages. Especially the use and function of proverbs in the Bible are seen as messages for a moral existence in God's world. A longer treatise on the proverb "Vox populi, vox Dei" is a fitting conclusion to this volume by a serious philologist with a moral message.

Richard Chenevix Trench's *Proverbs and Their Lessons* is thus an early comprehensive and comparative study of proverbs. Much can still be learned from his accessible lessons void of any pretentious jargon. It is therefore with much pleasure and excitement that I offer this reprint to the world of modern readers one hundred fifty years after Trench's original publication.

Burlington, Vermont   Wolfgang Mieder
Spring 2003

PROVERBS
AND THEIR LESSONS

By

RICHARD CHENEVIX TRENCH, D.D.

ARCHBISHOP OF DUBLIN

With Additional Notes and a Bibliography of Proverbs

By

A. SMYTHE PALMER, D.D.

Author of " The Folk and their Word-lore," etc.

LONDON

GEORGE ROUTLEDGE & SONS, LIMITED

NEW YORK: E. P. DUTTON & CO.

1905

EDITOR'S PREFACE

As in the previous volumes of this series, the editor's additions may be distinguished from the text of the author by the square brackets [thus] in which they are enclosed.

He has supplemented Archbishop Trench's work with some appendices on Ancient Proverbs and a fairly full bibliography of this interesting branch of literature. The foreign proverbs have also been translated into English.

AUTHOR'S PREFACE

It may be as well to state, that the lectures which are here published were never delivered as a complete course, but only one here and two there, as matter gradually grew under my hands ; yet so that very much the greater part of what is contained in this volume has been at one time or another actually delivered. Although I have always taken a lively interest in national proverbs, I had no intention at the first of making a book about them ; but only selected the subject as one which I thought, though I was not confident of this, might afford me sufficient material for a single lecture, which I had undertaken some time ago to deliver. I confess that I was at the time almost entirely ignorant of the immense number and variety of books bearing on the subject. Many of these I still know only by name. With some of the best, however, I have made myself acquainted, and by their aid, with the addition of such further material as I could myself furnish, these lectures have assumed their present shape ; and I publish them, because none of the works on proverbs which I know is exactly that book for all readers which I could have wished to see. Either they include matter which cannot be fitly placed before all—or they address themselves to the scholar alone, or if not so, are at any rate inaccessible to the mere English reader—or they contain bare lists of proverbs, with no endeavour to compare, illustrate, and explain them—or if they seek to explain, yet they do it without attempting to sound the depths, or measure the real significance, of that which they undertake to unfold. From these or other causes it has come to pass, that with a multitude of books, many of them admirable, on a subject so popular, there is no single one which is frequent in the hands of men. I will not deny that, with all the slightness and shortcomings of my own, I have still hoped to supply, at least for the present, this deficiency.

CONTENTS

PROVERBS AND THEIR LESSONS

THE FORM AND DEFINITION OF A PROVERB

It is very likely that for some of us proverbs have never attracted the notice which I am persuaded they deserve ; and from this it may follow that, when invited to bestow even a brief attention on them, we are in some doubt whether they will repay our pains. We think of them but as sayings on the lips of the multitude ; not a few of them have been familiar to us as far back as we can remember ; often employed by ourselves, or in our hearing, on slight and trivial occasions : and thus, from these and other causes, it may very well be, that, however sometimes one may have taken our fancy, we yet have remained blind in the main to the wit, wisdom, and imagination, of which they are full ; and very little conscious of the amusement, instruction, insight, which they are capable of yielding. Unless too we have devoted a certain attention to the subject, we shall not be at all aware how little those more familiar ones, which are frequent on the lips of men, exhaust the treasure of our native proverbs ; how many and what excellent ones remain behind, having now for the most part fallen out of sight ; or what riches in like kind other nations possess. We may little guess how many aspects of interest there are in which our own by themselves, and our own compared with those of other people, may be regarded.

And yet there is much to induce us to reconsider our judgment, should we be thus tempted to slight them, and to count them not merely trite, but trivial and unworthy of a serious attention. The fact that they please the people, and have pleased them for ages,—that they possess so vigorous a principle of life, as to have maintained their ground, ever new and ever young, through all the centuries of a nation's existence,—nay, that many of them have pleased not one nation only, but many, so that they have made themselves an home in the most different lands,—and further, that they have, not a few of them, come down to us from remotest antiquity*, borne safely upon the waters .of that great stream of time, which has swallowed so much beneath its waves,—all this, I think, may well make us pause, should we be tempted to turn away from them with anything of indifference or disdain.

And then further, there is this to be considered, that some of the greatest poets, the profoundest philosophers, the most learned scholars, the most genial writers in every kind, have delighted in them, have made large and frequent use of them,

* [The Proverbial Precepts of Ptah-hotep form a part of the oldest book of the world and date from about 3440 B.C. I give some of them in the Appendix, Note A].

have bestowed infinite labour on the gathering and elucidating of them.   In a fastidious age, indeed, and one of false refinement, they may go nearly or quite out of use among the so-called upper classes. No gentleman, says Lord Chesterfield, or ' no man of fashion ', as I think is his exact phrase, ' ever uses a proverb * '.   And with how fine a touch of nature Shakespeare makes Coriolanus, the man who, with all his greatness, is entirely devoid of all sympathy for the people, to utter his scorn *of them* in scorn of their proverbs, and of their frequent employment of these :

Hang 'em !
They said they were an hungry, sighed forth proverbs ;—
That, *hunger broke stone walls ;* that, *dogs must eat ;*
That, *meat was made for mouths ;* that, *the gods sent not
Corn for the rich men only ;*—with these shreds
They vented their complainings.

Coriolanus. Act I, sc. i.

But that they have been always dear to the true intellectual aristocracy of a nation, there is abundant evidence to prove†.   Take but these three names in evidence, which though few, are in themselves a host.   Aristotle made a collection of proverbs ; nor did he count that he was

* A similar contempt of them speaks out in the antithesis of the French Jesuit, Bouhours : Les proverbes sont les sentences du peuple, et les sentences sont les proverbes des honnêtes gens.

† [' The Proverbs of several Nations were much studied by Bishop Andrewes, and the reason he gave was, because by them he knew the minds of several Nations which is a brave thing ; as we count him a wise man that knows the minds and insides of men, which is done by knowing what is habitual to them.   Proverbs are habitual to a Nation, being transmitted from Father to Son '.— Selden, *Table-Talk,* 1689, p. 100 (ed. Arber)].

herein doing aught unworthy of his great reputation, however some of his adversaries may afterwards have made of the fact that he did so an
imputation against him.   He is said to have been
the first collector of them, though many afterwards followed in the same path.   Shakespeare
loves them so well, that besides often citing them,
and scattering innumerable covert illusions, rapid
side glances at them, which we are in danger of
missing unless at home in the proverbs of England,
several of his plays, as *Measure for Measure, All's
well that ends well,* have popular proverbs for their
titles.   And Cervantes, a name only inferior to
Shakespeare, has made very plain the affection
with which he regarded them.   Every reader of
Don Quixote will remember his squire, who sometimes cannot open his mouth but there drop from
it almost as many proverbs as phrases*.   I might
name others who have held the proverb in honour
—men who though they may not attain to these
first three, are yet deservedly accounted great ; as
Plautus, the most genial of Latin poets ; Rabelais
and Montaigne, the two most original of French
authors ; and how often Fuller, whom Coleridge
has styled the wittiest of writers, justifies this
praise in his witty employment of some old proverb : and no reader can thoroughly understand
and enjoy *Hudibras,* none but will miss a multitude of its keenest allusions, who is not thoroughly
familiar with the proverbial literature of England.

Nor is this all ; we may with reverence adduce
quite another name than any of these, the Lord

* [A collection of these was made by Mr. Ulick Ralph
Burke in a little work entitled *Sancho Panza's Proverbs.*]

himself, as condescending to employ such proverbs as He found current among his people. Thus, on the occasion of his first open appearance in the synagogue of Nazareth, He refers to the proverb, *Physician, heal thyself,* (Luke iv. 23,) as one which his hearers will perhaps bring forward against himself ; and again presently to another, *A prophet is not without honour but in his own country,* attested in his own history ; and at the well of Sychar He declares, ' Herein is that saying ', or that proverb, ' true, *One soweth and another reapeth* '. (John iv. 37.) But He is much more than a quoter of other men's proverbs ; He is a maker of his own. As all forms of human composition find their archetypes and their highest realization in Scripture, as there is no tragedy like Job, no pastoral like Ruth, no lyric melodies like the Psalms, so we should affirm no proverbs like those of Solomon, were it not that ' a greater than Solomon ' has drawn out of the rich treasure house of the Eternal Wisdom a series of proverbs more costly still. For indeed how much of our Lord's teaching, especially as recorded in the three first Evangelists, is thrown into this form ; and how many of his words have in this shape passed over as ' faithful sayings ' upon the lips of men ; and so doing, have fulfilled a necessary condition of the proverb, whereof we shall have presently to speak.

But not urging this testimony any further,—a testimony too august to be lightly used, or employed merely to swell the testimonies of men— least of all, men of such ' uncircumcised lips ' as, with all their genius, were more than one of those whom I have named,—and appealing only to the latter, I shall be justified, I feel, in affirming that whether we listen to those single voices which make a silence for themselves, and are heard through the centuries and their ages, or to that great universal voice of humanity, which is wiser even than these (for it is these, with all else which is worthy to be heard added to them), there is here a subject, which those whose judgments should go very far with us have not accounted unworthy of their serious regard.

And I am sure if we bestow on them ourselves even a moderate share of attention, we shall be ready to set our own seal to the judgment of wiser men that have preceded us here. For, indeed, what a body of popular good sense and good feeling, as we shall then perceive, is contained in the better, which is also the more numerous, portion of them ; what a sense of natural equity, what a spirit of kindness breathes out from many of them ; what prudent rules for the management of life, what shrewd wisdom, which though not *of* this world, is most truly *for* it, what frugality, what patience, what perseverance, what manly independence, are continually inculcated by them. What a fine knowledge of the human heart do many of them display ; what useful, and not always obvious, hints do they offer on many most important points, as on the choice of companions, the bringing up of children, the bearing of prosperity and adversity, the restraint of all immoderate expectations. And they take a yet higher range than this ; they have their ethics, their theology, their views of man in his highest relations of all, as man with his fellow man, and man with his Maker. Be these always correct or not, and I should be very far from affirming that they always are so, the student of humanity, he who because he is a man counts nothing human to be alien to him, can never without wilfully foregoing an important document, and one which would have helped him often in his studies, altogether neglect or pass them by.

But what, it may be asked, before we proceed further, is a proverb ? Nothing is harder than a definition. While on the one hand there is for the most part no easier task than to detect a fault or flaw in the definitions of those who have gone before us, nothing on the other is more difficult than to propose one of our own, which shall not also present a vulnerable side. Some one has said that these three things go to the constituting of a proverb, *shortness*, *sense*, and *salt*. In brief pointed sayings of this kind, the second of the qualities enumerated here, namely *sense*, is sometimes sacrificed to alliteration. I would not affirm that it is so here : for the words are not ill spoken, though they are very far from satisfying the rigorous requirements of a definition, as will be seen when we consider what the writer intended by his three *esses*, which it is not hard to understand. The proverb, he would say, must have *shortness* ; it must be succinct, utterable in a breath. It must have *sense*, not being, that is, the mere small talk of conversation, slight and trivial, else it would perish as soon as born, no one taking the trouble to keep it alive. It must have *salt*, that is, besides its good sense, it must in its manner and outward form be pointed and pungent, having a sting in it, a barb which shall not suffer it to drop lightly from the memory *. Yet, regarded as a definition, this of the triple *s* fails, as I have said ; it indeed errs both in defect and excess.

Thus in demanding *shortness*, it errs in excess. It is indeed quite certain that a good proverb will be short, as short, that is, as is compatible with the full and forcible conveying of that which it intends. Brevity, ' the soul of wit ', will be eminently the soul of a proverb's wit ; it will contain, according to Fuller's definition, ' much matter decocted into few words '. Oftentimes it will consist of two, three, or four, and these sometimes monosyllabic, words. Thus *Extremes meet ;—Right wrongs no man ;—Forewarned, forearmed ;—* with a thousand more †. But still shortness is

---

* Compare with this Martial's so happy epigram upon epigrams, in which everything runs exactly parallel to that which has been said above :

Omne epigramma sit instar apis ; sit aculeus illi,
    Sint sua mella, sit et corporis exigui ;

which may be indifferently rendered thus :

Three things must epigrams, like bees, have all—
Its sting, its honey, and its body small.

† The very shortest proverb which I know in the world is this German : Voll, toll [' Full, dull ', i.e. senseless] ; which sets out very well the connexion between fulness and folly, pride and abundance of bread. In that seeking of extreme brevity noted above, they sometimes become exceedingly elliptical, (although this is the case more with the ancient than with the modern,) so much so as to omit even the vital element of the sentence, the verb. Thus : Χρήματ' ἀνήρ :—Sus Minervam ;—Fures clamorem ; Meretrix pudicam ;—Amantes amentes [i.e. ' Money (makes) the man '; 'A sow (teach) Minerva', the goddess of Wisdom, much like our ' Teach your grandmother to suck eggs ' ; ' Thieves and noise ' ; ' A harlot

only a relative term, and it would perhaps be more accurate to say that a proverb must be *concise*, cut down, that is, to the fewest possible words ; condensed, quintessential wisdom *. But that, if only it fulfil this condition of being as short as possible, it need not be absolutely very short, there are sufficient examples to prove. Thus Freytag has admitted the following, which indeed hovers on the confines of the fable, into his great collection of Arabic proverbs : *They said to the camel-bird*, [i.e., the ostrich,] ' *Carry* ' : *it answered*, ' *I cannot, for I am a bird* '. *They said*, ' *Fly* ' ; *it answered*, ' *I cannot, for I am a camel* '. This could not be shorter, yet, as compared with the greater number of proverbs, is not short †. Even so the *sense* and *salt*, which are ascribed to the proverb as other of its necessary conditions, can hardly be said to be such ; seeing that flat, saltless proverbs, though comparatively rare, there certainly are ; while yet, be it remembered, we are not considering now what are the ornaments of a *good* proverb, but the essential marks of all.

And then moreover it errs in defect ; for it has

and a chaste woman ' ; ' Lovers (ever) silly, or ' lovers, duffers '.]

 * This is what Aristotle means when he ascribes συντομία [conciseness]—which in another place he opposes to the ὄγκος λέξεως [cumbrous diction]—to it.

 † Let serve for further proof this eminently witty old German proverb, which, despite its apparent length, has not forfeited its character as such. I shall prefer to leave it in the original : Man spricht, an viererlei Leuten ist Mangel auf Erden : an Pfaffen, sonst dürfte einer nit 6 bis 7 Pfruenden ; an Adelichen, sonst wollte nit jeder Bauer ein Junker sein ; an Huren, sonst würden die Handwerk Eheweiber und Nunnen nit treiben ; an Juden, sonst würden Christen nit wuchern.

plainly omitted one quality of the proverb, and that the most essential of all—I mean *popularity*, acceptance and adoption on the part of the people. Without this popularity, without these suffrages and this consent of the many, no saying, however brief, however wise, however seasoned with salt, however worthy on all these accounts to have become a proverb, however fulfilling all other its conditions, can yet be esteemed as such. This popularity, omitted in that enumeration of the essential notes of the proverb, is yet the only one whose presence is absolutely necessary, whose absence is fatal to the claims of any saying to be regarded as such.

Those, however, who have occupied themselves with the making of collections of proverbs have sometimes failed to realize this to themselves with sufficient clearness, or at any rate have not kept it always before them ; and thus it has come to pass, that many collections include whatever brief sayings their gatherers have anywhere met with which to them have appeared keenly, or wisely, or wittily spoken * ; while yet a multitude of these

* When Erasmus, after discussing and rejecting the definitions of those who had gone before him, himself defines the proverb thus, Celebre dictum, scitâ quâpiam novitate insigne [a saying in frequent use marked by some shrewdness and originality,] it appears to me that he has not escaped the fault which he has blamed in others—that, namely, of confounding the accidental adjuncts of a *good* proverb with the necessary conditions of *every* proverb. In rigour the whole second clause of the definition should be dismissed, and Celebre dictum alone remain. Better Eifelein (*Sprichwörter des deutschen Volkes*, Friburg, 1840, p. x.) : Das Sprichwort ist ein mit öffentlichem Gepräge ausgemünzter Saz, der seinen Curs und anerkannten Werth unter dem Volke hat

have never received their adoption into the great
family of proverbs, or their rights of citizenship
therein : inasmuch as they have never passed into
general recognition and currency, have no claim
to this title, however just a claim they may have
on other grounds to our admiration and honour.
For instance, this word of Goethe's, ' A man need
not be an architect to live in an house ', seems to
me to have every essential of a proverb, saving only
that it has not passed over upon the lips of men.
It is a saying of manifold application ; an universal law is knit up in a particular example ; I mean
that gracious law in the distribution of blessing,
which does not limit our use and enjoyment of
things by our understanding of them, but continually makes the enjoyment much wider than the
knowledge ; so that it is not required that one be
a botanist to have pleasure in a rose, nor a critic
to delight in *Paradise Lost,* nor a theologian to
taste all the blessings of Christian faith, nor, as he
expresses it, an architect to live in an house. And
here is an inimitable saying of Schiller's : ' Heaven
and earth fight in vain against a dunce ' ; yet it is
not a proverb, because his alone ; although abundantly worthy to have become such * ; moving as
it does in the same line with, though far superior
to, the Chinese proverb, which itself also is good :

[i.e., The proverb is a coinage of the popular mint
and owns its currency and acknowledged value to the
people. Compare with this the very similar definition
of Howell given below, p. 14.]

* It suggests, however, the admirable Spanish proverb,
spoken no doubt out of the same conviction : Dios me
dè contienda, con quien me entienda [God grant me
to argue with those who understand me.]

One has never so much need of his wit, as when he has to do with a fool.

Or to take another example still more to the point. James Howell, a prolific English writer of the earlier half of the seventeenth century, one certainly meriting better than that almost entire oblivion into which his writings have fallen, occupied himself much with proverbs ; and besides collecting those of others, he has himself set down ' five hundred new sayings, which in tract of time may serve for proverbs to posterity '. As was to be expected, they have not so done ; for it is not after this artificial method that such are born ; yet many of these proverbs in expectation are expressed with sense and felicity ; for example : ' Pride is a flower that grows in the devil's garden ' ; as again, the selfishness which characterizes too many proverbs is not ill reproduced in the following : ' Burn not thy fingers to snuff another man's candle ' ; and there is at any rate good theology in the following : ' Faith is a great lady, and good works are her attendants ' ; and in this : ' The poor are God's receivers, and the angels are his auditors '. Yet for all this, it would be inaccurate to quote these as proverbs, (and their author himself, as we have seen, did not do more than set them out as proverbs upon trial,) inasmuch as they have remained the private property of him who first devised them, never having passed into general circulation ; which until men's sayings have done, maxims, sentences, apothegms, aphorisms they may be, and these of excellent temper and proof, but proverbs as yet they are not.

It is because of this, the popularity inherent in a genuine proverb, that from such an one in a certain sense there is no appeal. You will not suppose me to intend that there is no appeal from its wisdom, truth, or justice ; from any word of man's there may be such ; but no appeal from it, as most truly representing a popular conviction. Aristotle, who in his ethical and political writings often finds very much more than this in it, always finds this. It may not be, it very often will not be, an universal conviction which it expresses, but ever one popular and widespread. So far indeed from an universal, very often over against the one proverb there will be another, its direct antagonist ; and the one shall belong to the kingdom of light, the other to the kingdom of darkness. *Common fame is seldom to blame ;* here is the baser proverb, for as many as drink in with greedy ears all reports to the injury of their neighbours ; being determined from the first that they *shall* be true. But it is not left without its compensation : ' *They say so* ', *is half a liar ;* here is the better word with which *they* may arm themselves, who count it a primal duty to close their ears against all such unauthenticated rumours to the discredit of their brethren. *The noblest vengeance is to forgive* : here is the godlike proverb on the manner in which wrongs should be recompensed ; *He who cannot revenge himself is weak, he who will not is vile* *, here is the devilish. These lines occur in a sonnet which Howell has prefixed to his collection of proverbs :

* Chi non può fare sua vendetta è debile, chi non vuole è vile.

The people's voice the voice of God we call ;
  And what are proverbs but the people's voice ?
  Coined first, and current made by common choice ?
Then sure they must have weight and truth withal ;

It will follow from what has just been said, that, true in the main, they yet cannot be taken without certain qualifications and exceptions *.

Herein in great part the force of a proverb lies, namely, that it has already received the stamp of popular allowance. A man might produce, (for what another has done, he might do again,) something as witty, as forcible, as much to the point, of his own ; which should be hammered at the instant on his own anvil. Yet still it is not ' the wisdom of many ' ; it has not stood the test of experience ; it wants that which the other already has, but which it only after a long period can acquire—the consenting voice of many and at different times to its wisdom and truth. A man employing a ' proverb of the ancients ', (1 Sam. xxiv. 13,) is not speaking of his own, but uttering a faith and conviction very far wider than that of himself or of any single man ; and it is because he is so doing that they, in Lord Bacon's words, ' serve not only for ornament and delight, but also

---

* Quintilian's words (*Inst.* 5. 11. 41), which are to the same effect, must be taken with the same exception ; Neque enim durâssent hæc in æternum, nisi vera omnibus viderentur [They would not last for ever had they not been universally considered true]; and also Don Quixote's : Paréceme me, Sancho, que no ay refrán que no sea verdadéro, porque todas son sentencias sacadas de la misma experiencia, madre de las ciencias todas [Methinks, Sancho, that there is no proverb that is not true, because they are all judgments drawn from the same experience which is the mother of all knowledge].

for active and civil use ; as being the edge tools of speech which cut and penetrate the knots of business and affairs '. The proverb has in fact the same advantage over the word now produced for the first time, which for present currency and value has the recognised coin of the realm over the rude unstamped ore newly washed from the stream, or dug up from the mine. This last *may* possess an equal amount of fineness ; but the other has been stamped long ago, has already passed often from man to man, and found free acceptance with all * : it inspires therefore a confidence which the ruder metal cannot at present challenge. And the same satisfaction which the educated man finds in referring the particular matter before him to the universal law which rules it, a plainer man finds in the appeal to a proverb. He is doing the same thing ; taking refuge, that is, as each man so gladly does, from his mere self and single fallible judgment, in a larger experience and in a wider conviction.

And in all this which has been urged lies, as it seems to me, the explanation of a sentence of an ancient grammarian, which at first sight appears to contain a bald absurdity, namely, that a proverb is ' a saying without an author '. For, however, without a *known* author it may, and in the majority of cases it must be, still, as we no more believe in the spontaneous generation of proverbs

* Thus in a proverb about proverbs, the Italians say, with a true insight into this its prerogative : Il proverbio *s'invecchia,* e chi vuol far bene, vi si specchia [The proverb is of old standing and he who would do well will make it his looking-glass.]

than of anything else, an author every one of them must have had. It might, however, and it often will have been, that in its utterance the author did but *precipitate* the floating convictions of the society round him ; he did but clothe in happier form what others had already felt, or even already uttered ; for often a proverb has been in this aspect, ' the wit of one, and the wisdom of many '. And further, its constitutive element, as we must all now perceive, is not the utterance on the part of the one, but the acceptance on the part of the many. It is *their* sanction which first makes it to be such ; so that every one who took or gave it during the period when it was struggling into recognition may claim to have had a share in its production ; and in this sense without any single author it may have been. From the very first the people will have vindicated it for their own. And thus though they do not always analyse the compliment paid to them in the use of their pro-verbs, they always feel it ; they feel that a writer or speaker using these is putting himself on their ground, is entering on their region, and they wel-come him the more cordially for this *.

Let us now consider if some other have not sometimes been proposed as essential notes of the

---

* The name which the proverb bears in Spanish points to this fact, that popularity is a necessary condition of it.   This name is not *proverbio*, for that in Spanish signifies an apothegm, an aphorism, a maxim ; but *refran*, which is *a referendo*, from the frequency of its repetition ; yet see Diez, *Etymol. Wörterbuch*, p. 284.   The etymology of the Greek παροιμία is somewhat doubtful, but it too means probably a *trite, wayside* saying.

proverb, which yet are in fact accidents, such as may be present or absent without affecting it vitally. Into an error of this kind they have fallen, who have claimed for the proverb, and made it one of its necessary conditions, that it should be a figurative expression. A moment's consideration will be sufficient to disprove this. How many proverbs, such as *Haste makes waste ;—Honesty is the best policy*, with ten thousand more, have nothing figurative about them. Here again the error has arisen from taking that which belongs certainly to very many proverbs, and those oftentimes the best and choicest, and transferring it, as a necessary condition, to all. This much of truth they who made the assertion certainly had ; namely, that the employment of the concrete instead of the abstract is one of the most frequent means by which it obtains and keeps its popularity ; for so the proverb makes its appeal to the whole man— not to the intellectual faculties alone, but to the feelings, to the fancy, or even to the imagination, as well, stirring the whole man to pleasurable activity.

By the help of an instance or two we can best realize to ourselves how great an advantage it thus obtains for itself. Suppose, for example, one were to content himself with saying, ' He may wait till he is a beggar, who waits to be rich by other men's deaths,' would this trite morality be likely to go half so far, or to be remembered half so long, as the vigorous comparison of this proverb : *He who waits for dead men's shoes may go barefoot* * ? Or again, what were ' All men are

* The same, under a different image, in Spanish :

T.E.P.   C

mortal ', as compared with the proverb : *Every door may be shut but death's door?* Or let one observe : ' More perish by intemperance than are drowned in the sea '; is this anything better than a painful, yet at the same time a flat truism ? But let it be put in this shape : *More are drowned in the beaker than in the ocean * ;* or again in this : *More are drowned in wine and in beer than in water †:* (and these both are German proverbs,) and the assertion assumes quite a different character. There is something that lays hold on us now. We are struck with the smallness of the cup as set against the vastness of the ocean, while yet so many more deaths are ascribed to that than to this ; and further with the fact that literally none are, and none could be, drowned in the former, while multitudes perish in the latter. In the justifying of the paradox, in the extricating of the real truth from the apparent falsehood of the statement, in the answer to the appeal made here to the imagination,—an appeal and challenge which, unless it be responded to, the proverb must remain unintelligible to us,—in all this there is a process of mental activity, oftentimes so rapidly exercised as scarcely to be perceptible, yet not the less carried on with a pleasurable excitement ‡.

Larga soga tira, quien por muerte agena suspira [He drags a long rope who longs for the death of another].
   * Im Becher ersaufen mehr als im Meere.
   † In Wein und Bier ertrinken mehr denn im Wasser.
   ‡ Here is the explanation of the perplexity of Erasmus. Deinde fit, *nescio quo pacto*, ut sententia proverbio quasi vibrata feriat acrius auditoris animum, et aculeos quosdam cogitationum relinquat infixos [So it comes to pass somehow that an aphorism discharged in a proverb

Let me mention now a few other of the more frequent helps which the proverb employs for obtaining currency among men, for being listened to with pleasure by them, for not slipping again from their memories who have once heard it ;— yet helps which are evidently so separable from it, that none can be in danger of affirming them essential parts or conditions of it. Of these rhyme is the most prominent. It would lead me altogether from my immediate argument, were I to enter into a disquisition on the causes of the charm which rhyme has for us all ; but that it does possess a wondrous charm, that we *like* what is *like*, is attested by a thousand facts, and not least by the circumstance that into this rhyming form a very great multitude of proverbs, and those among the most widely current, have been thrown. Though such will probably at once be present to the minds of all, yet let me mention a few : *Good mind, good find ;—Wide will wear, but tight will tear ;—Truth may be blamed, but cannot be shamed ;—Little strokes fell great oaks ;—Women's jars breed men's wars ;—A king's face should give grace ;—East, west, home is best ;—Store is no sore ; —Slow help is no help ;—Who goes a-borrowing goes a-sorrowing ;—*with many more, uniting, as you will observe several of them do, this of rhyme with that which I have spoken of before, namely, extreme brevity and conciseness *.

strikes the mind of the hearer more sharply and leaves some stings of thought deeply implanted].

* So, too, in other languages ; Qui prend, se rend ;— Qui se loue, s'emboue ;—Chi và piano, và sano, e và lontano ;—Chi compra terra, compra guerra ;—Quien se muda, Dios le ayuda ;—Wie gewonnen, so zerronnen ;

Alliteration, which is nearly allied to rhyme, is another of the helps whereof the proverb largely avails itself. Alliteration was at one time an important element in our early English versification ; it almost promised to contend with rhyme itself, which should be the most important ; and perhaps, if some great master in the art had arisen, might have retained a far greater hold on English poetry than it now possesses. At present it is merely secondary and subsidiary. Yet it cannot be called altogether unimportant ; no master of melody despises it ; on the contrary, the greatest, as in our days Tennyson, make the most frequent,

and the Latin medieval ;—Qualis vita, finis ita ;—Via crucis, via lucis ;—Uniti muniti [He who takes loses his liberty ;—Who praises himself bemires himself ;—Who goes softly goes safely and goes far ;—He who buys land buys strife ;—Reform yourself and God will help you ;—Lightly won lightly spent ;—As is the life such is its end ;—The way of the cross the way of light ;—Union is strength]—We sometimes regard rhyme as a modern invention, and to the modern world no doubt the discovery of all its capabilities, and the consequent large application of it belongs. But proverbs alone would be sufficient to show that in itself it is not modern, however restricted in old times the employment of it may have been. For instance, there is a Greek proverb to express that men learn by their sufferings more than by any other teaching : Παθή-ματα, μαθήματα ([Sufferings are lessons] Herodotus, i, 207); one which in the Latin, Nocumenta, documenta, or, Quæ nocent, docent, finds both in rhyme and sense its equivalent ; to both of which evidently the inducement lay in the chiming and rhyming words. Another rhyming Greek proverb which I have met, Πλησμονή, ἐπιλησμονή, implying that fulness of blessings is too often accompanied with forgetfulness of their Author (*Deut.* 8. 11–14), is, I fancy, not ancient—at least does not date further back than Greek Christianity. The sentiment would imply this, and the fact that the word ἐπιλησμονή does not occur in classical Greek would seem to be decisive upon it.

though not always the most obvious, use of it. In the proverb you will find it of continual recurrence, and where it falls, as, to be worth anything, it must, on the key-words of the sentence, of very high value. Thus : *Frost and fraud both end in foul ;—Like lips, like lettuce* * *;—Meal and matins minish no way ;—Who swims on sin, shall sink in sorrow ;—No cross, no crown ;—Out of debt, out of danger ;—Do on hill as you would do in hall* † *;* that is, Be in solitude the same that you would be in a crowd. I will not detain you with further examples of this in other languages ; but such occur, and in such numbers that it seems idle to quote them, in all ; I will only adduce, in concluding this branch of the subject, a single Italian proverb, which in a remarkable manner unites all three qualities of which we have been last treating, brevity, rhyme, and alliteration : *Traduttori, traditori ;* one which we might perhaps reconstitute in English thus : *Translators, traitors ;* so untrue, for the most part, are they to the genius of their original, to its spirit, if not to its letter, and frequently to both ; so do they *surrender*, rather than *render*, its meaning ; not *turning*, but only *overturning*, it from one language to another ‡.

A certain pleasant exaggeration, the use of the

---

* So in Latin : Nil sole et sale utilius ; and in Greek Σῶμα, σῆμα [There's nothing more useful than light and salt. The body is a tomb (or a token)].

† [The exclamation of M. Crassus on seeing an ass eating thistles—' Similem habent labra lactucam '].

‡ This is St. Jerome's pun, who complains that the Latin versions of the Greek Testament current in the Church in his day were too many of them not *versiones*, but *eversiones* [Compare Ger. *uebersetzen*, to translate].

figure hyperbole, a figure of natural rhetoric which Scripture itself does not disdain to employ, is a not unfrequent engine with the proverb to procure attention, and to make a way for itself into the minds of men.   Thus the Persians have a proverb : *A needle's eye is wide enough for two friends ; the whole world is too narrow for two foes.*   Again, of a man whose good luck seems never to forsake him, so that from the very things which would be another man's ruin he extricates himself not merely without harm, but with credit and with gain, the Arabs say : *Fling him into the Nile, and he will come up with a fish in his mouth ;* while of such a Fortunatus as this the Germans have a proverb : *If he flung a penny on the roof, a dollar would come down to him* * ; as, again, of the man in the opposite extreme of fortune, to whom the most unlikely calamities, and such as beforehand might seem to exclude one another, befall, they say : *He would fall on his back, and break his nose.*

In all this which I have just traced out, in the fact that the proverbs of a language are so frequently its highest bloom and flower, while yet so much of their beauty consists often in curious felicities of diction pertaining exclusively to some single language, either in a rapid conciseness to which nothing tantamount exists elsewhere, or in rhymes which it is hard to reproduce, or in alliterations which do not easily find their equivalents, or in other verbal happinesses such as these, lies

---

* Würf er einen Groschen aufs Dach, fiel ihm Ein Thaler herunter ;—compare another : Wer Glück hat, dem kalbet ein Ochs [For the man who is lucky his ox has a calf ; (see F. E. Hulme, *Proverb Lore*, p. 9)].

the difficulty which is often felt, which I shall myself often feel in the course of these lectures, of
transferring them without serious loss, nay, sometimes the impossibility of transferring them at all
from one language to another *. Oftentimes, to
use an image of Erasmus †, they are like those
wines, (I believe the Spanish Valdepeñas is one,)
of which the true excellence can only be known by
those who drink them in the land which gave them
birth. Transport them under other skies, or,
which is still more fatal, empty them from vesse

* Thus in respect of this German proverb :
　　　Stultus und *Stolz*
　　　Wachset aus Einem Holz ;
its transfer into any other languages is manifestly impossible.
　　　[' Folly and Pride
　　　Grow side by side '
(lit. on the same tree). The two words are indeed from
the same root, *stal*, fixed firm, whence Lat. *stultus*, slow,
dull, stupid, foolish, and *stolidus*, It. *stolto*, old Fr. *estout*,
　stout,' Ger. *stolz*, ' Stout ' formerly bore the meaning
of proud as in the A.V. (Is. xlvi. 12 ; Dan. vii. 20 ; Mal.
iii. 13), and the proverb, ' You stout and I stout, who'll
carry the dirt out ? '] The same may be affirmed of
another, commending stay-at-home habits to the wife :
Die *Hausfrau* soll nit sein eine *Ausfrau* [A house-wife
should be a house-keeper]; or again of this beautiful
Spanish one : La *verdad* es siempre *verde* [Truth is an
ever-green].
　† Habent enim hoc peculiare pleraque proverbia, ut in
eâ linguâ sonare postulant in quâ nata sunt ; quod si in
alienum sermonem demigrârint, multum gratiæ decedat.
Quemadmodum sunt et vina quædam quæ recusant ex-
portari, nec germanam saporis gratiam obtineant, nisi
in his locis in quibus proveniunt [Most proverbs have
this peculiarity that they sound best in their native
tongue, but if they are translated into another language
they lose much of their beauty ; just as some wines
cannot stand exportation, and only give their proper
delicacy of flavour in the places where they are produced.]

to vessel, and their strength and flavour will in great part have disappeared in the process.

Still this is rather the case, where we seek deliberately, and only in a literary interest, to translate some proverb which we admire from its native language into our own or another. Where, on the contrary, *it has transferred itself*, made for itself a second home, and taken root a second time in the heart and affections of a people, in such a case one is continually surprised at the instinctive skill with which it has found compensations for that which it has been compelled to let go ; it is impossible not to admire the unconscious skill with which it has replaced one vigorous idiom by another, one happy rhyme or play on words by its equivalent ; and all this even in those cases where the extremely narrow limits in which it must confine itself allow it the very smallest liberty of selection. And thus, presenting itself equally finished and complete in two or even more languages, the internal evidence will be quite insufficient to determine which of its forms we shall regard as the original, and which as a copy. For example, the proverb at once German and French, which I can present in no comelier English dress than this,

> Mother's truth
> Keeps constant youth ;

but which in German runs thus,

> *Mutter-treu*
> *Wird täglich neu ;*

and in French,

> *Tendresse maternelle*
> *Toujours se renouvelle :*

appears to me as exquisitely graceful and tender in the one language as in the other * ; while yet so much of its beauty depends on the form, that beforehand one could hardly have expected that the charm of it would have survived its transfer to the second language, whichever that may be, wherein it found an home. Having thus opened the subject, I shall reserve its further development for the lectures which follow.

* [Mr. W. K. Kelly adduces as worthy parallels the Scotch, ' The mither's breath is aye sweet,' and the Spanish, ' No hay tal madre como la que pare,' ' There's no mother like her who bore us ' (*Proverbs of all Nations*, p. 26). See an article on ' The Philosophy of Proverbs,' in D'Israeli's *Curiosities of Literature*, p. 385 seq., ed. 1838.

A Tuscan proverb says, 'Many give me bread, but not like my mother '—Giusti, *Raccolta di Proverbi Toscani*].

THE GENERATION OF PROVERBS

In my preceding lecture I occupied your attention with the form and definition of a proverb ; let us proceed in the present to realize to ourselves, so far as this may be possible, the processes by which a nation gets together the great body of its proverbs, the sources from which it mainly derives them, and the circumstances under which such as it makes for itself of new, had their birth and generation.

And first, I would call to your attention the fact that a vast number of its proverbs a people does not make for itself, but finds ready made to its hands : it enters upon them as a part of its intellectual and moral inheritance. The world has now endured so long, and the successive generations of men have thought, felt, enjoyed, suffered, and altogether learned so much, that there is an immense stock of wisdom which may be said to belong to humanity in common, being the gathered fruits of all this its experience in the past. Even Aristotle, more than two thousand years ago, could speak of proverbs as ' the fragments of an elder wisdom, which, on account of their brevity and aptness, had amid a general wreck and ruin been preserved.' These, the common property of the civilized world, are the original stock with which each nation starts ; these, either orally handed down to it, or made its own by those of its earlier writers who brought it into living communication with the past.   Thus, and through these channels, a vast number of Greek, Latin, and medieval proverbs live on with us, and with all the modern nations of the world.   [Appendix, Notes B, C.]

It is, indeed, oftentimes a veritable surprise to discover the venerable age and antiquity of a proverb, which we have hitherto assumed to be quite a later birth of modern society.   Thus we may perhaps suppose that well-known word which forbids the too accurate scanning of a present, *One must not look a gift horse in the mouth*, to be of English extraction, the genuine growth of our own soil.   I will not pretend to say how old it may be, but it is certainly as old as Jerome, a Latin father of the fourth century ; who, when some found fault with certain writings of his, replied with a tartness which he could occasionally exhibit, that they were voluntary on his part, free-will offerings, and with this quoted the proverb, *that it did not behove to look a gift horse in the mouth ;* and before it comes to us, we meet it once more in one of the rhymed Latin verses, which were such great favourites in the middle ages.   [See Appendix, p. 145.]

Si quis dat mannos, ne quære in dentibus annos
[If one gives you a nag don't look at his teeth for his age].

Again, *Liars should have good memories* is a saying which probably we assume to be modern ; yet it is very far from so being.   The same Jerome, who, I may observe by the way, is a very great quoter of proverbs, and who has preserved some that would not otherwise have descended to us *, speaks of one as ' unmindful of the *old* proverb, *Liars should have good memories* ' †, and we find it ourselves in a Latin writer a good deal older than him ‡. So too I was certainly surprised to discover the other day that our own proverb : *Good company on a journey is worth a coach,* has come down to us from the ancient world §.

Having lighted just now on one of those Latin rhymed verses, let me by the way guard against an error about them, into which it would be very easy to fall. I have seen it suggested that these, if not the source *from* which, are yet the channels *by* which, a great many proverbs have reached us. I should greatly doubt it. This much we may conclude from the existence of proverbs in this shape, namely, that since these rhymed or

* Thus is it, I believe, with, Bos lassus fortius figit pedem [A tired ox plants his foot the heavier] ; a proverb with which he warns the younger Augustine not to provoke a contest with him, the weary, but therefore the more formidable, antagonist.

† Oblitus *veteris* proverbii : mendaces memores esse oportere. Let me quote here Fuller's excellent unfolding of this proverb : 'Memory in a liar is no more than needs. For first lies are hard to be remembered, because many, whereas truth is but one ; secondly, because a lie cursorily told takes little footing and settled fastness in the teller's memory, but prints itself deeper in the hearers, who take the greater notice because of the improbability and deformity thereof ; and one will remember the sight of a monster longer than the sight of an handsome body. Hence comes it to pass that when the liar hath forgotten himself, his auditors put him in mind of the lie and take him therein.'

‡ Quintilian, *Inst.* 1. 4.

§ Comes facundus in viâ pro vehiculo est [A chatty companion on the road is as good as a carriage].

leonine verses went altogether out of fashion at the revival of a classical taste in the fifteenth century, such proverbs as are found in this form may be affirmed with a tolerable certainty to date at least as far back as that period ; but not that in all or even in a majority of cases, this shape was their earliest. Oftentime the proverb in its more popular form is so greatly superior to the same in this its Latin monkish dress, that the latter by its tameness and flatness betrays itself at once as the inadequate translation, and we cannot fail to regard the other as the genuine proverb. Many of them are ' so essentially Teutonic, that they frequently appear to great disadvantage in the Latin garb which has been huddled upon them '*. Thus, when we have on one side the English, *Hungry bellies have no ears,* and on the other the Latin,

> Jejunus venter non audit verba libenter.
> [A fasting stomach makes a bad listener],

who can doubt that the first is the proverb, and the second only its versification ? Or who would hesitate to affirm that the old Greek proverb, *A rolling stone gathers no moss* †, may very well have come to us without the intervention of the medieval Latin,

> Non fit hirsutus lapis hinc atque inde volutus ?
> [A stone rolled hither and thither is never mossed over].

* Kemble, *Salomon and Saturn,* p. 56.
† Compare :—
[' Selden moseth the marbleston that men ofte treden'.
> Langland, *Piers Powman,* A. x. 101.
' Syldon mossyth the stone
That oftyn ys tornnyd and winde'.
> *Book of Precedence,* ab. 1406, p. 39 (E.E.T.S.).
' The stone that is rouling can gather no mosse.'—
Tusser, *Five Hundred Pointes of Good Husbandrie.*]

And the true state of the case comes out still more clearly, where there are *two* of these rhymed Latin equivalents for the one popular proverb, and these quite independent of each other. So it is in respect of our English proverb : *A bird in the hand is worth two in the bush ;* which appears in this form :

Una avis in dextrâ melior quam quatuor extra ;
[One bird in the hand is better than four outside it

And also in this :

Capta avis est pluris quam mille in gramine ruris.
[A captured bird is worth a thousand on the green.]

Who can fail to see here two independent attempts to render the same saying ? Sometimes the Latin line confesses itself to be only the rendering of a popular word ; thus is it with the following :

Ut dicunt multi, cito transit lancea stulti ;

in other words : *A fool's bolt is soon shot *.*

Then, besides this derivation from elder sources, from the literat re of nations which as such now no longer exist, besides this process in which a people are merely receivers and borrowers, there is also at somewhat later periods in its life a mutual interchange between it and other nations growing up beside, and cotemporaneously with it, of their own several inventions in this kind ; a free

---

*['Sottes bolt is sone shote'
(A fool's bolt is soon shot),
Proverbs of Hendyng, ab. 1280.
Compare the Spanish 'Quien poco sabe presto lo reza (He who knows little soon tells it), and the French 'De fol juge brève sentence' (A foolish judge gives brief sentence).]

giving and taking, in which it is often hard, and oftener impossible, to say which is the lender and which the borrower. Thus the quantity of proverbs not drawn from antiquity, but common to all, or nearly all of the modern European languages, is very great. The ' solidarity ' (to use a word which it is in vain to strive against) of all the nations of Christendom comes out very noticeably here.

There is indeed nothing in the study of proverbs, in the attribution of them to their right owners, in the arrangement and citation of them, which creates a greater perplexity than the circumstances of finding the same proverb in so many different quarters, current among so many different nations. In quoting it as of one, it often seems as if we were doing wrong to many, while yet it is almost, or oftener still altogether, impossible to determine to what nation it first belonged, so that others drew it at second hand from that one ;—even granting that any form in which we now possess it is really its oldest of all. More than once this fact has occasioned a serious disappointment to the zealous collector of the proverbs of his native country. Proud of the rich treasures which in this kind it possessed, he has very reluctantly discovered on a fuller investigation of the whole subject, how many of these which he counted native, the peculiar heirloom and glory of his own land, must at once and without hesitation be resigned to others, who can be shown beyond all doubt to have been in earlier possession of them : while in respect of many more, if his own nation can put in a claim to them as well as others, yet he is compelled to feel that it can put in no better than, oftentimes not so good as, many competitors *.

This single fact, which it is impossible to question, that nations are thus continually borrowing proverbs from one another, is sufficient to show that, however the great body of those which are the portion of a nation may be, some almost as old as itself, and some far older, it would for all this be a serious mistake to regard the sum of them as a closed account, neither capable of, nor actually receiving, addition—a mistake of the same character as that sometimes made in regard to the *words* of a language. So long as a language is living, it will be appropriating foreign words, putting forth new words of its own. Exactly in the same way, so long as a people have any vigorous energies at work in them, are acquiring any new experiences of life, are forming any new moral convictions, for the new experiences and convictions new utterances will be found ; and some of the happiest of these will receive that stamp of general allowance which shall constitute them proverbs. And this fact makes it little likely that the collections which exist in print, and certainly not the earlier ones, will embrace all the proverbs in actual circulation. They preserve, indeed, many others ; all those which have now become obsolete, and which would, but for them, have been forgotten ; but there are not a few, as I imagine, which, living on the lips of men, have yet never found their way into books, however worthy to have done so ; and this, either

* Kelly, in the preface to his very useful collection of Scotch proverbs, describes his own disappointment at making exactly such a discovery as this.

because the sphere in which they circulate has continued always a narrow one, or that the occasions which call them out are very rare, or that they, having only lately risen up, have not hitherto attracted the attention of any who cared to record them. It would be well, if such as take an interest in the subject, and are sufficiently well versed in the proverbial literature of their own country to recognise such unregistered proverbs when they meet them, would secure them from that perishing, which, so long as they remain merely oral, might easily overtake them ; and would make them at the same time, what all *good* proverbs ought certainly to be, the common heritage of all *.

* The pages of the excellent *Notes and Queries* would no doubt be open to receive such, and in them they might be safely garnered up. That there are such proverbs to reward him who should carefully watch for them, is abundantly proved by the immense addition, which, as I shall have occasion hereafter to mention, a Spanish scholar was able to make to the collected proverbs, so numerous before, of Spain. Nor do there want other indications of the like kind. Thus, the editor of very far the best modern collection of German proverbs, records this one, found, as he affirms, in no preceding collection, and by himself never heard but once, and then from the lips of an aged lay servitor of a monastery in the Black Forest : *Offend one monk, and the lappets of all cowls will flutter as far as Rome* (Beleidigestu einen Münch, so knappen alle Kuttenzipfel bis nach Rom) ; and yet who can doubt that we have a genuine proverb here, and one excellently expressive of the common cause which the whole of the monastic orders, despite their inner dissensions, made ever, when assailed from without, with one another ? It is very easy to be deceived in such a matter, and one must be content often to be so ; but the following, which is current in Ireland, I have never seen in print : ' *The man on the dyke always hurls well* ' ; the looker-on at a game of hurling, seated indolently on the wall, always imagines that he could improve

And as new proverbs will be born from life and from life's experience, so too there will be another fruitful source of their further increase, namely, the books which the people have made heartily their own. Portions of these they will continually detach, most often word for word ; at other times wrought up into new shapes with that freedom which they claim to exercise in regard of whatever they thus appropriate to their own use. These, having detached, they will give and take as part of their current intellectual money. Thus ' *Evil communications corrupt good manners* ' * (1 Cor. xv. 33,) is word for word a metrical line from a Greek comedy. It is not probable that St. Paul had ever read this comedy, but the words for their truth's sake had been taken up into the common speech of men ; and not as a citation, but as a proverb, he uses them. And if you will, from this point of view, glance over a few pages of one of Shakespeare's more popular dramas,—Hamlet, for example, —you will be surprised, in case your attention has never been called to this before, to note how much has in this manner been separated from it, that it might pass into the every-day use and service of man ; and you will be prepared to estimate higher than ever what he has done for his fellow country-men, the ' possession for ever ' which his writings have become for them. And much no doubt is passing even now from favourite authors into the flesh and blood of a nation's moral and intellectual

on the strokes of the actual players, and, if you will listen to him, would have played the game much better than they ; a proverb of sufficiently wide application.

* Φθείρουσιν ἤθη χρῆσθ' ὁμιλίαι κακαί.

life ; and as 'household words', as parts of its proverbial philosophy, for ever incorporating itself therewith. We have a fair measure of an author's true popularity, I mean of the real and lasting hold which he has taken on his nation's heart, in the extent to which it has been thus done with his writings.

There is another way in which additions are from time to time made to the proverbial wealth of a people. Some event has laid strong hold of their imagination, has stirred up the depths of their moral consciousness ; and this they have gathered up for themselves, perhaps in some striking phrase which was uttered at the moment, or in some allusive words, understood by everybody, and which at once summon up the whole incident before their eyes.

Sacred history furnishes us with one example at the least of the generation in this wise of a proverb. That word, ' *Is Saul also among the prophets ?* ' is one of which we know the exact manner in which it grew to be a ' proverb in Israel '. When the son of Kish revealed of a sudden that nobler life which had hitherto been slumbering in him, alike un- dreamt of by himself and by others, took his part and place among the sons of the prophets, and, borne along in their enthusiasm, praised and prophesied as they did, showing that he was indeed turned into another man, then all that knew him be- forehand said one to another, some probably in sin- cere astonishment, some in irony and unbelief, ' Is Saul also among the prophets ? ' And the question they asked found and finds its application so often

as any reveals of a sudden, at some crisis of his life,
qualities for which those who knew him the longest
had hitherto given him no credit, a nobleness which
had been latent in him until now, a power of taking
his place among the worthiest and the best, which
none until now had at all deemed him to possess.
It will, of course, find equally its application, when
one does not step truly, but only affects suddenly
to step, into an higher school, to take his place in
a nobler circle of life, than that in which hitherto
he has moved.

Another proverb, and one well known to the
Greek scholar, *The cranes of Ibycus* *, had its rise
in one of those remarkable incidents, which, wit-
nessing for God's inscrutable judgments, are eagerly
grasped by men. The story of its birth is indeed
one to which so deep a moral interest is attached,
that I shall not hesitate to repeat it, even at the
risk that Schiller's immortal poem on the subject,
or it may be the classical studies of some here
present, may have made it already familiar to a
portion of my hearers. Ibycus, a famous lyrical
poet of Greece, journeying to Corinth, was assailed
by robbers : as he fell beneath their murderous
strokes he looked round, if any witnesses or avengers were nigh. No living thing was in sight, save
only a flight of cranes soaring high over head. He
called on them, and to them committed the
avenging of his blood. A vain commission, as it
might have appeared, and as no doubt it did to the
murderers appear. Yet it was not so. For these,
sitting a little time after in the open theatre at
Corinth, beheld this flight of cranes hovering above

* Αἱ Ἰβύκου γέρανοι.

them, and one said scoffingly to another, ' Lo,
there, the avengers of Ibycus ! ' The words were
caught up by some near them ; for already the
poet's disappearance had awakened anxiety and
alarm. Being questioned, they betrayed themselves, and were led to their doom ; and *The cranes
of Ibycus* passed into a proverb, very much as our
Murder will out,* to express the wondrous leadings
of God whereby continually the secretest thing of
blood is brought to the open light of day.

Gold of Toulouse † is another of these proverbs in
which men's sense of a God verily ruling and judg-
ing the earth has found its embodiment. The
Consul Q. S. Cæpio had taken the city of Toulouse
by an act of more than common perfidy and
treachery ; and possessed himself of the immense

[* Similarly Plutarch tells of one Bessus, who having
murdered his father was seen to trample on a nest of
young swallows because they *would* keep crying ' parri-
cide ! ' (*Opera, De Serâ Num. Vind.* viii. 190). And
Alonso, in *The Tempest*, who thinks he has drowned his
son, exclaims :—' Methought the billows spoke and told
me of it ; the winds did sing it to me, and the thunder,
that deep and dreadful organ-pipe, pronounced the name
of Prosper ' (iii. 3, 96–99). So the Hebrew Preacher :—
' Curse not the king, no not in thy thought, and curse
not the rich in thy bedchamber ; for a bird of the air
shall carry the voice, and that which hath wings shall
tell the matter ' (*Eccles.* x. 20).
    ' Wretched is he who thinks of doing ill,
      His evil deeds long to conceal and hide ;
    For though the voice and tongues of men be still,
      By fowls and beasts his sins shall be descried.
    And God oft worketh by his secret will,
      That sin itself, the sinner so doth guide,
      That of his own accord without request,
      He makes his wicked doings manifest.'
                         Sir J. Harington, 1591.]
  † Aurum Tolosanum ; see C. Merivale, *Fall of the
Roman Republic*, p. 63.

hoards of wealth stored in the temples of the Gaulish deities. From this day forth he was so hunted by calamity, all extremest evils and disasters, all shame and dishonour, fell so thick on himself and all who were his, and were so traced up by the moral instinct of mankind to this accursed thing which he had made his own, that any wicked gains, fatal to their possessor, acquired this name ; and of such a one it would be said ' He has gold of Toulouse '.

Another proverb, which in English has run into the following posy, *There's many a slip 'twixt the cup and the lip*, descends to us from the Greeks, having a very striking story connected with it : A master treated with extreme cruelty his slaves who were occupied in planting and otherwise laying out a vineyard for him ; until at length one of them, the most misused, prophesied that for this his cruelty he should never drink of its wine. When the first vintage was completed, he bade this slave to fill a goblet for him, which taking in his hand he at the same time taunted him with the non-fulfil- ment of his prophecy. The other replied with words which have since become proverbial : as he spake, tidings were hastily brought of a huge wild boar that was wasting the vineyard. Setting down the untasted cup, the master went out to meet the wild boar, and was slain in the encounter, and thus the proverb, *Many things find place between the cup and lip*, arose *.

---

* Πολλὰ μεταξύ πέλει κύλικος καὶ χείλεος ἄκρου. The Latin form of the proverb, Inter os et offam, will not adapt itself to this story. [' Saepe audivi inter os atque offam multa intervenire posse ' (M. Cato, in A. Gellius, xiii. 17. See H. E. P. Platt, *Alia*, p. 18).

A Scotch proverb, *He that invented the Maiden, first hanselled it,* is not altogether unworthy to rank with these. It alludes to the well-known historic fact that the Regent Morton, the inventor of a new instrument of death called 'The Maiden', was himself the first upon whom the proof of it was made. Men felt, to use the language of the Latin poet, that 'no law was juster than that the artificers of death should perish by their own art', and embodied their sense of this in the proverb.

Memorable words of illustrious men will frequently not die in the utterance, but pass from mouth to mouth, being still repeated with complacency, till at length they have received their adoption into the great family of national proverbs. Such were the gnomes or sayings of the Seven Wise Men of Greece, supposing them to have been indeed theirs, and not ascribed to them only after they had obtained universal currency and acceptance. So too a saying, attributed to Alexander the Great, may very well have arisen on the occasion, and under the circumstances, to which its birth is commonly ascribed. When some of his officers reported to him with something of dismay the innumerable multitudes of the Persian hosts which

Mr. Hulme quotes from a 1586 collection: 'Many thingis happen betwene the cupe and the lyp' (*Proverb Lore,* p. 97), which also occurs in B. Jonson's *Tale of a Tub,* 1633 ; Horace's, 'Multa cadunt inter calicem supremaque labra' ; compare in French, 'Entre la bouche et le verre le vin souvent tombe à terre' (Between the mouth and the glass the wine often falls to the ground), 'De la main à la bouche se perd souvent la soupe' (Between hand and mouth the soup is often spilt), and 'Vin versé n'est pas avalé' (Wine poured out is not swallowed).]

were advancing to assail him, the youthful Macedonian hero silenced them and their apprehensions with the reply : *One butcher does not fear many sheep ;* not in this applying an old proverb, but framing a new, and one admirably expressive of the confidence which he felt in the immeasurable superiority of the Hellenic over the barbarian man ; —and this word, having been once set on foot by him, has since lived on, and that, because the occasions were so numerous on which a word like this would find its application.

And taking occasion from this royal proverb, let me just observe by the way, that it would be a great mistake to assume, though the error is by no means an uncommon one, that because proverbs are popular, they have therefore originally sprung from the bosom of the populace.   What was urged in my first lecture of their popularity was not at all intended in this sense ; and the sound common sense, the wit, the wisdom, the right feeling, which are their *predominant* characteristics, alike contradict any such supposition.   They spring rather from the sound healthy kernel of the nation, whether in high place or in low ; and it is surely worthy of note, how large a proportion of those with the generation of which we are acquainted, owe their existence to the foremost men of their time, to its philosophers, its princes, and its kings ; as it would not be difficult to show.   And indeed the evil in proverbs testifies to this quite as much as the good.   Thus the many proverbs in almost all modern tongues expressing scorn of the ' villain ' are alone sufficient to show that for the most part they are very far from having their birth quite in the lower regions of society, but reflect much oftener the prejudices and passions of those higher in the social scale.

Let me adduce another example of the proverbs which have thus grown out of an incident, which contain an allusion to it, and are only perfectly intelligible when the incident itself is known. It is this Spanish : *Let that which is lost be for God ;* one the story of whose birth is thus given by the leading Spanish commentator on the proverbs of his nation :—The father of a family, making his will and disposing of his goods upon his death-bed, ordained concerning a certain cow which had strayed, and had been now for a long time missing, that, if it were found, it should be for his children, if otherwise for God : and hence the proverb, *Let that which is lost be for God*, arose. The saying was not one to let die ; it laid bare with too fine a skill some of the subtlest treacheries of the human heart ; for, indeed, whenever men would give to God only their lame and their blind, that which costs them nothing, that from which they hope no good, no profit, no pleasure for themselves, what are they saying in their hearts but that which this man said openly, *Let that which is lost be for God.*

This subject of the generation of proverbs, upon which I have thus touched so slightly, is yet one upon which whole volumes have been written. Those who have occupied themselves herein have sought to trace historically the circumstances out of which various proverbs have sprung, and to which they owe their existence ; that so by the analogy of these we might realize to ourselves the rise of others whose origins lie out of our vision, obscure and unknown. No one will deny the interest of the subject : it cannot but be most interesting to preside thus at the birth of a saying which has lived on and held its ground in the world, and has not ceased, from the day it was first uttered, to be more or less of a spiritual or intellectual force among men. Still the cases where this is possible are exceeding rare, as compared with the far greater number where the first birth is veiled, as is almost all birth, in mystery and obscurity. And indeed it could scarcely be otherwise. The great majority of proverbs are foundlings, the happier foundlings of a nation's wit, which the collective nation has refused to let perish, has taken up and adopted for its own. But still, as must be expected to be the case with foundlings, they can for the most part give no distinct account of themselves. They make their way, relying on their own merits, not on those of their parents and authors ; whom they have forgotten ; and who seem equally to have forgotten them, or, at any rate, fail to claim them. Not seldom, too, when a story has been given to account for a proverb's rise, it must remain a question open to much doubt, whether the story has not been subsequently imagined for the proverb, rather than that the proverb has indeed sprung out of history *.

The proverb having thus had its rise from life,

---

* Livy's account of ' Cantherium in fossâ ' [' a hack in the ditch,' said of one in a helpless plight], and of the manner in which it became a rustic proverb in Italy, (23, 47,) is a case in point, where it is very hard to give credit to the parentage which has been assigned to the saying. See Döderlein's *Lat. Synonyme*, v. 4. p. 289.

however it may be often impossible to trace that
rise, will continually turn back to life again ; it
will attest its own practical character by the frequency with which it will present itself for use, and
will have been actually used upon earnest and
important occasions ; throwing its weight into one
scale or the other at some critical moment, and
sometimes with decisive effect. I have little doubt
that with knowledge sufficient one might bring
together a large collection of instances wherein, at
significant moments, the proverb has played its
part, and, it may be, very often helped to bring
about issues, of which all would acknowledge the
importance.

In this aspect, as having been used at a great
critical moment, and as part of the moral influence
brought to bear on that occasion for effecting a
great result, no proverb of man's can be compared
with that one which the Lord used when He met
His future Apostle, but at this time His persecutor,
in the way, and warned him of the fruitlessness and
folly of a longer resistance to a might which must
overcome him, and with still greater harm to himself, at the last : *It is hard for thee to kick against
the pricks* *. (Acts xxvi. 14.) It is not always
observed, but yet it adds much to the fitness
of this proverb's use on this great occasion, that it
was already, even in that heathen world to which
originally it belonged, predominantly used to note
the madness of a striving on man's part against the

---

* Σκληρόν σοι πρὸς κέντρα λακτίζειν. [So πρὸς κέντρα μὴ
λάκτιζε μὴ παίσας μογῆς (Aesch. *Agam.* 1624)—kick not
against the goads lest you suffer from the collision—and
Pindar, *Pyth.* 2. 173; in Latin, ' Aduorsum stimulum
calcas ' (Terence, *Phorm.* 1. 2, 28).]

superior power of the gods ; for so we find it in the chief passages of heathen antiquity in which it occurs *.

I must take the second illustration of my assertion from a very different quarter, passing at a single stride from the kingdom of heaven to the kingdom of hell, and finding my example there. We are told then, that when Catherine de Medicis desired to overcome the hesitation of her son Charles the Ninth, and draw from him his consent to the massacre, afterwards known as that of St. Bartholomew, she urged on him with effect a proverb which she had brought with her from her own land, and assuredly one of the most convenient maxims for tyrants that was ever framed : *Sometimes clemency is cruelty, and cruelty clemency.*

Later French history supplies another and more agreeable illustration. At the siege of Douay, Louis the Fourteenth found himself with his suite unexpectedly under a heavy cannonade from the besieged city. I do not believe that Louis was deficient in personal courage, yet, in compliance with the entreaties of most of those around him, who urged that he should not expose so important a life, he was about, in somewhat unsoldierly and unkingly fashion, immediately to retire ; when M. de Charost, drawing close to him, whispered the well-known French proverb in his ear : *The wine is drawn : it must be drunk* †. The king remained

---

* Æschylus, *Prom. Vinct.* 322 ; Euripides, *Bacch.* 795 ; Pindar, *Pyth.* 2. 94–96. The image is of course that of the stubborn ox, which when urged to go forward, recalcitrates against the sharp-pointed iron goad, and, already wounded, thus only wounds itself the more.

† Le vin est versé ; il faut le boire.

exposed to the fire of the enemy a suitable period, and it is said ever after held in higher honour than before the counsellor who had with this word saved him from an unseemly retreat. Let this on the generation of proverbs, with the actual employment which has been made of them, for the present suffice.

THE PROVERBS OF DIFFERENT NATIONS COMPARED

'THE genius, wit, and spirit of a nation are discovered in its proverbs'—this is Lord Bacon's well-worn remark ; although, indeed, only well-worn because of its truth. ' In them ', it has been further said, ' is to be found an inexhaustible source of precious documents in regard of the interior history, the manners, the opinions, the beliefs *, the customs of the people among whom they have

* The writer might have added, the superstitions ; for proverbs not a few involve and rest on popular superstitions, and a collection of these would be curious and in many ways instructive. Such, for instance, is the Latin, (it is, indeed, also Greek) : *A serpent, unless it devour a serpent, grows not to a dragon ;* (Serpens, nisi serpentem comederit, non fit draco) ; which Lord Bacon moralizes so shrewdly : ' The folly of one man is the fortune of another ; for no man prospers so suddenly as by other men's errors '. Such again is the old German proverb : *The night is no man's friend ;* (Die Nacht ist keines Menschen Freund ;) which rests, as Grimm has so truly observed (*Deutsche Mythol.* p. 713) on the wide-spread feeling in the northern mythologies, of the night as an unfriendly and, indeed, hostile power to man. [Etymologically the ' night ' is that which *noieth* or injures ; *nox (noct-s)* nocet ; la *nuit* nuit. See my *Word-hunter's Note-book*, pp. 199 *seq.*] And such, too, the French : *A Sunday's child dies never of the plague ;* (Qui naît le dimanche, jamais ne meurt de peste).

had their course ' *. Let us put these assertions to the proof, and see how far in this people's or in that people's proverbs, their innermost heart speaks out to us ; how far the comparison of the proverbs of one nation with those of others may be made instructive to us ; what this comparison will tell us severally about each. This only I will ask, ere we enter upon the subject, that if I should fail here in drawing out anything strongly characteristic, if the proverbs regarded from this point of view should not seem to reveal to you any of the true secrets of national life, you will not therefore misdoubt those assertions with which my lecture opened ; or assume that these documents would not yield up their secret, if questioned aright ; but only believe that the test has been unskilfully applied ; or, if you will, that my brief limits have not allowed me to make that clear, which with larger space I might not have wholly failed in doing.

I am very well aware that in following upon this track, one is ever liable to deceive oneself, to impose upon others, picking out and adducing such proverbs as conform to a preconceived theory, passing over those which would militate against it. Quite allowing that there is such a danger which needs to be guarded against, and also that there are a multitude of these sayings which cannot be made to illustrate differences, for they rest on the

---

* We may adduce further the words of Salmasius : Argutæ hæ brevesque loquendi formulæ suas habent ve-neres, et genium cujusque gentis penes quam celebrantur, atque acumen ostendunt. [These pungent and short forms of speaking have a grace of their own, and display the genius and sharpness of the people amongst whom they pass current.]

broad foundation of the universal humanity,
underlying and deeper than that which is peculiar
and national, I am yet persuaded that enough
remain, and such as may with perfect good faith
be adduced, to confirm these assertions ; I am
convinced that we *may* learn from the proverbs
current among a people, what is nearest and
dearest to their hearts, the aspects under which
they contemplate life, how honour and dishonour
are distributed among them, what is of good,
what of evil report in their eyes, with very much
more which it can never be unprofitable to know.

To begin, then, with the proverbs of Greece.
That which strikes one most in the study of these,
and which, the more they are studied, the more fills
the thoughtful student with wonder, is the evidence
they yield of a leavening through and through of
the entire nation with the most intimate knowledge
of its own mythology, history, and poetry. The
infinite multitude of slight and fine allusions to the
legends of their gods and heroes, to the earlier
incidents of their own history, to the Homeric
narrative, the delicate side glances at all these
which the Greek proverbs constantly embody *,
assume an acquaintance, indeed a familiarity, with
all this on their parts among whom they passed
current, which almost exceeds belief. In many
and most important respects, the Greek proverbs
considered as a whole are inferior to those of many

* Thus ’Αΐδος κυνῆ—"Απληστος πίθος. — ’Ιλιὰς κακῶν.
[‘ A Hades cap ’ (i.e. a tarn-cap, which makes one in-
visible) ; ‘ a jar that cannot be filled ’ (like that of the
Danaides) ; ‘ An Iliad of woes.’]

nations of modern Christendom. This is nothing wonderful ; Christianity would have done little for the world, would have proved very ineffectual for the elevating, purifying, and deepening of man's life, if it had been otherwise. But, with all this, as being testimony to the high intellectual training of the people who employed them, to a culture not restricted to certain classes, but which must have been diffused through the whole nation, no other collection can bear the remotest comparison with this.

It is altogether different with the Roman proverbs. These, the genuine Roman, the growth of their own soil, are very far fewer in number than the Greek, as was indeed to be expected from the far less subtle and less fertile genius of the people. Hardly any of them are legendary or mythological ; which again agrees with the fact that the Italian pantheon was very scantily peopled as compared with the Greek. Very few have much poetry about them, or any very rare delicacy or refinement of feeling. In respect of love indeed, not the Roman only, but Greek and Roman alike, are immeasurably inferior to those which many modern nations could supply. Thus a proverb of such religious depth and beauty as our own, *Marriages are made in heaven*, it would have been quite impossible for all heathen antiquity to have produced, or even remotely to have approached *.
In the setting out not of love, but of friendship,

---

* This Greek proverb on love is the noblest of the kind which I remember : Μουσικὴν ἔρως διδάσκει, κἄν τις ἄμουσος ᾖ τὸ πρίν [Love teaches culture (gives a liberal education)—even if one was before uncultured].

T.E.P.   E

and of the claims which it makes, the blessings which it brings, is exhibited whatever depth and tenderness they may have *. This indeed, as has been truly observed †, was only to be expected, seeing how much higher an ideal of that existed than of this, the full realization of which was reserved for the modern Christian world. Yet the Roman proverbs are not without other substantial merits of their own. A vigorous moral sense speaks out in many ‡ ; and even when this is not so prominent, they wear often a thoroughly old Roman aspect ; being business-like and practical, frugal and severe, wise saws such as the elder Cato must have loved, such as must have been often upon his lips § ; while in the number that relate to farming, they bear singular witness to that strong and lively interest in agricultural pursuits, which was so remarkable a feature in the old Italian life ‖.

* In this respect the Latin proverb, Mores amici noveris, non oderis [You may know your friend's character and not dislike him], on which Horace has furnished so exquisite a comment (*Sat.* i. 3, 24–93), and which finds its graceful equivalent in the Italian, Ama l'amico tuo con il difetto suo (Love your friend with his fault), is worthy of all admiration.

† By Zell, in his slight but graceful treatise, *On the proverbs of the ancient Romans* (*Ferienschriften*, v. 2, p. 1–96).

‡ Thus, Noxa caput sequitur ;—Conscientia, mille testes.

[The injury falls on one's own pate ; Conscience is as a thousand witnesses].

§ He has preserved for us that very sensible and at the same time truly characteristic one, Quod non opus est, asse carum est [What you don't want is dear at a penny].

‖ These are two or three of the most notable—the first against ' high farming,' which it is strange if it has not

It will not be possible to pass under even this hastiest review more than two or three of the modern families of proverbs. Let us turn first to the proverbs of Spain. I put these in the foremost rank, because the Spanish literature, poor in many provinces wherein other literatures are rich, is probably richer in this province than any other in the world, certainly than any other in the western world ; and this I should be inclined to believe both as respects the quantity and the quality *. In respect of quantity, the mere number of Spanish proverbs is astonishing. A collection I have been using while preparing these lectures, contains between seven and eight thousand, and yet does not contain all ; for I have searched it in vain for several with which from other sources I had become acquainted. Nay, it must be very far indeed from exhausting the entire stock, seeing that there exists a manuscript collection brought together by a distinguished Spanish scholar, in which the pro-

---

been appealed to in the modern controversy on the subject : Nihil minus expedit quam agrum optime colere (Pliny, *H. N.*, 6. 18) [Nothing is more unprofitable than high cultivation]. Over against this, however, we must set another warning] against the attempt to farm with insufficient capital : Oportet agrum imbecilliorem esse quam agricolam [The ground ought to be poorer than the farmer]; and yet another, on the liberal answer which the land will make to the pains and cost bestowed on it : Qui arat olivetum, rogat fructum ; qui stercorat, exorat ; qui cædit, cogit [He who digs up his olive-yard, asks fruit of it ; he who manures, demands it ; he who prunes, exacts it].

 * This was the judgment of Salmasius, who says : Inter Europæos Hispani in his excellunt, Itali vix cedunt, Galli proximo sequuntur intervallo [Of the Europeans the Spaniards excel in these, the Italians are hardly inferior to them, the French come next].

verbs have attained to the almost incredible amount
of from five and twenty to thirty thousand *.

And in respect of their quality, it needs only
to call to mind some of those, so rich in humour,
so double-shotted with homely sense, wherewith
the Squire in *Don Quixote* adorns his discourse ;
being oftentimes indeed not the fringe and border,
but the main woof and texture of it : and then, if
we assume that the remainder are not altogether
unlike these, we shall, I think, feel that it would
be difficult to rate them more highly than they
deserve. And some are in a loftier vein ; for taking,
as we have a right to do, Cervantes himself as the
truest exponent of the Spanish character, we
should be prepared to trace in the proverbs of
Spain a grave thoughtfulness, a stately humour,
to find them breathing the very spirit of chivalry
and honour, and indeed of freedom too ;—for in
Spain, as throughout so much of Europe, it is
despotism, and not freedom, which is new. Nor
are we disappointed in these our expectations.
How eminently chivalresque, for instance, the following : *White hands cannot hurt* †. What a grave
humour lurks in this : *The ass knows well in*

* What may have become of this collection I know
not ; but it was formerly in Richard Heber's library (see
the *Catalogue*, v. 9. no. 1697). Juna Yriarte was the collector, and in a note to the *Catalogue* it is stated that he
devoted himself with such eagerness to the bringing of it
to the highest possible state of completeness, that he
would give his servants a fee for any new proverb they
brought him ; while to each, as it was inserted in his list,
he was careful to attach a memorandum of the quarter
from which it came ; and if this was not from books but
from life, an indication of the name, the rank, and condition in life of the person from whom it was derived.

† Las manos blancas no ofenden.

whose face he brays *. What a stately apathy, how proud a looking of calamity in the face, speaks out in the admonition which this one contains : *When thou seest thine house in flames, approach and warm thyself by it* † ; what a spirit of freedom, which refuses to be encroached on even by the highest, is embodied in another : *The king goes as far as he may, not as far as he would* ‡ ; what Castilian pride in the following : *Every layman in Castile might make a king, every clerk a pope.* The Spaniard's contempt for his peninsular neighbours finds its emphatic utterance in another : *Take from a Spaniard all his good qualities, and there remains a Portuguese.*

We may too, I think, remark how a nation will occasionally in its proverbs indulge in a fine irony upon itself, and show that it is perfectly aware of its own weaknesses, follies, and faults. This the Spaniards must be allowed to do in their proverb, *Succours of Spain, either late, or never* §. However largely and confidently promised, these *succours of Spain* either do not arrive at all, or only arrive after the opportunity in which they could have served has passed away. Certainly any one who reads the despatches of England's Great Captain during the Peninsular War will find in almost every page of them that which abundantly justifies this proverb, will own that those who made it read themselves aright, and could not have designated broken pledges, unfulfilled promises of aid, tardy

---

* Bien sabe el asno en cuya cara rebozna.
† Quando vierás tu casa quemar, llega te á escalentar.
‡ El Rey va hasta do puede, y no hasta do quiere.
§ Socorros de España, ó tarde, ó nunca.

and thus ineffectual assistance, by an happier title than *Succours of Spain*. And then again what a fearful glimpse of those blood feuds which, having once begun, seem as if they could never end, blood touching blood, and violence evermore provoking its like, have we in the following : *Kill, and thou shalt be killed, and they shall kill him who kills thee* *.

The Italians also are eminently rich in proverbs ; and yet if ever I have been tempted to retract or seriously to modify what I shall have occasion by-and-by to affirm in regard of a nobler life and spirit as predominating in proverbs, it has been after the study of some Italian collection. ' The Italian proverbs ', it has been said not without too much reason, though perhaps also with overmuch severity, ' have taken a tinge from their deep and politic genius, and their wisdom seems wholly concentrated in their personal interests. I think every tenth proverb in an Italian collection is some cynical or some selfish maxim, a book of the world for worldlings ' †. Certainly many of them are shrewd enough, and only too shrewd ; ' ungracious,' inculcating an universal suspicion, teaching to look everywhere for a foe, to expect, as the Greeks said, a scorpion under every stone, glorifying artifice and cunning as the true guides and only safe leaders through the perplexed labyrinth of life ‡, and altogether seeming dictated as by the very spirit of Machiavel himself.

* Matarás, y matarte han, y matarán á quien te matará.
† *Curiosities of Literature*, p. 391. **London** : 1838.
‡ These may serve as examples : Chi ha sospetto, di rado è in difetto.—Fidarsi è bene, ma non fidarsi è meglio.

And worse than this is the glorification of revenge which speaks out in too many of them. I know nothing of its kind calculated to give one a more shuddering sense of horror than the series which might be drawn together of Italian proverbs on this matter ; especially when we take them with the commentary which Italian history supplies, and which shows them no empty words, but the deepest utterances of the nation's heart. There is no misgiving in these about the right of entertaining so deadly a guest in the bosom ; on the contrary, one of them, exalting the sweetness of revenge, declares, *Revenge is a morsel for God* *. There is nothing in them, (it would be far better if there were,) of blind and headlong passion, but rather a spirit of deliberate calculation, which makes the blood run cold. Thus one gives this advice : *Wait time and place to act thy revenge, for it is never well done in a hurry* † ; while another proclaims an immortality of hatred, which no spaces of intervening time shall have availed to weaken : *Revenge of an hundred years old hath still its sucking teeth* ‡. We may well be thankful

---

—Da chi mi fido, mi guardi Iddio ; da chi non mi fido, mi guarderò io.—Con arte e con inganno si vive mezzo l'anno ; con inganno e con arte si vive l'altra parte [He who suspects is seldom without occasion.—Trust is good, but distrust is better.—From those I trust God guard me, from those I trust not I will guard myself.— By skill and fraud one can live half the year, by fraud and skill one can live the remainder.]

* Vendetta, boccon di Dio.

† Aspetta tempo e loco à far tua vendetta, che la non si fa mai ben in fretta. Compare another : Vuoi far vendetta del tuo nemico, governati bene ed è bell' e fatta.

‡ Vendetta di cent' anni ha ancor i lattaiuoli.

that we have in England, at least as far as I am
aware, no sentiments parallel to these, embodied as
the permanent convictions of the national mind.

How curious again is the confession which speaks
out in another Italian proverb, that the mainte-
nance of the Romish system and the study of
Holy Scripture cannot go together. It is this :
With the Gospel one becomes an heretic *. No doubt
with the study of the Word of God one does become an heretic, in the Italian sense of the word ;
and therefore it is only prudently done to put all
obstacles in the way of that study, to assign three
years' and four years' imprisonment with hard
labour to as many as shall dare to peruse it ; yet
certainly it is not a little remarkable that such a
confession should have embodied itself in the
popular utterances of the nation.

But while it must be freely owned that the
charges brought just now against the Italian proverbs are sufficiently borne out by too many, they
are not all to be included in the common shame.
Very many there are not merely of a delicate
refinement of beauty, as this, expressive of the
freedom in regard of *thine* and *mine* which will
exist between true friends : *Friends tie their purses
with a spider's thread* †; of a subtle wisdom which

---

* Con l'Evangelo si diventa eretico. [The author,
following D'Israeli, *Curios. of Literature*, 1839, p. 394,
seems to have put a mistaken interpretation on this proverb, which originally ran, ' Con l'Evangelo talvolta si
diventa eretico,' ' With the Gospel one sometimes becomes
a heretic.' The true meaning is that even the best things
may be corrupted and turned to evil, as the sweetest wine
makes the sourest vinegar. See Giusti, *Raccolta*, 1853,
and W. R. Kelly, *Proverbs of All Nations*, p. 158.]

† Gli amici legono la borsa con un filo di ragnatelo.

has *not* degenerated into cunning and deceit ; but also of a nobler stamp ; honour and honesty, plain dealing and uprightness, have here their praises too, and are not seldom pronounced to be in the end more than a match for all cunning and deceit. How excellent in this sense is the following : *For an honest man half his wits is enough, the whole are too little for a knave* *; the ways, that is, of truth and uprightness are so simple and plain, that a little wit is abundantly sufficient for those that walk in them ; the ways of falsehood and fraud are so perplexed and tangled, that sooner or later all the wit of the cleverest rogue will not preserve him from being entangled therein. How often and how wonderfully has this found its confirmation in the lives of evil men ; so true it is, to employ another proverb and a very deep one from the same quarter, that *The devil is subtle, yet weaves a coarse web* †.

Again, what description of Egypt as it now is, or indeed generally of the East, could set us at the heart of its moral condition, could make us to understand all which long centuries of oppression and misrule have made of it and of its people, what could do this so effectually as the collection of Arabic proverbs now current in Egypt, which the traveller Burckhardt gathered, and which, after his

---

* Ad un uomo dabbene avanza la metà del cervello ; ad un tristo non basta ne anche tutto.

† Jeremy Taylor appears to have found much delight in the proverbs of Italy. In the brief footnotes which he has appended to the *Holy Living* alone I counted five and twenty such, to which he makes more or less remote allusion in the text. There is an excellent article on ' Tuscan Proverbs ' in *Fraser's Magazine,* Jan. 1857.

death, were published with his name * ?   In other
books, others describe the modern Egyptians, but
here they unconsciously describe themselves.   The
selfishness, the utter extinction of all public spirit,
the servility, which no longer as with an inward
shame creeps into men's acts, but utters itself
boldly as the avowed law of their lives, the sense
of the oppression of the strong, of the insecurity of
the weak, and, generally, the whole character of life,
alike outward and inward, as poor, mean, sordid,
and ignoble, with only a few faintest glimpses
of that romance which one usually attaches to the
East ; all this, as we study these documents, rises up
before us in truest, though in painfullest, outline.

Thus only in a land where rulers, being evil themselves, feel all goodness to be their instinctive foe,
and themselves therefore entertain an instinctive
hostility to it, where they punish but never reward,
where not to be noticed by them is the highest
ambition of those under their yoke, in no other
land could a proverb like the following, *Do no
good, and thou shalt find no evil,* have ever come
to the birth.   How settled a conviction that wrong,
and not right, was the lord paramount of the world
must have grown up in men's spirits, before such a
word as this, (I know of no sadder one,) could have
found utterance from their lips †.

I have taken a wide circuit of nations ; with the
proverb of a people nearer home I must bring

---

* *Arabic Proverbs of the Modern Egyptians.*   London :
1830.

† Yet this very mournful collection of Burckhardt's
possesses at least one very beautiful proverb on the all-
conquering power of love : *Man is the slave of beneficence.*

this branch of the subject to an end. It is one, and a very characteristic one, which the poet Spenser, who long dwelt in Ireland, records as current in his time among the Irish; in which were contained their offer of service to their native chiefs, with a statement of what they expected in return: *Spend me, and defend me.* Their leaders in all times have taken them only too well at their word in respect of the first half of the proverb, and have not failed prodigally to *spend* them; although their undertakings to *defend* have issued exactly as must ever issue all promises on the part of others to defend men from those evils, from which none can really protect them but themselves.

Other families of proverbs would each of them tell its own tale, give up its own secret; but I must not seek from this point of view to question them further. I would rather bring now to your notice that even where they do not spring, as they cannot all, from the centre of a people's heart, nor declare to us the secretest things which are there, but dwell more on the surface of things, in this case also they have often local or national features, which to study and trace out may prove both curious and instructive. Of how many, for example, we may note the manner in which they clothe themselves in an outward form and shape, borrowed from, or suggested by, the peculiar scenery or circumstances or history of their own land; so that they could scarcely have come into existence, not certainly in the shape which they now wear, anywhere besides. Thus our own, *Make hay while the sun shines*, is truly English, and could have had its birth only under such variable skies as ours,—not, at any rate, in those southern lands where, during the summer time at least, the sun always shines. In the same way there is a fine Cornish proverb in regard of obstinate wrongheads, who will take no counsel except from calamities, who dash themselves to pieces against obstacles, which with a little prudence and foresight they might easily have avoided. It is this : *He who will not be ruled by the rudder, must be ruled by the rock* *. It sets us at once upon some rocky and wreck-strewn coast ; we feel that it could never have been the proverb of an inland people. And this, *Do not talk Arabic in the house of a Moor* †, —that is, because there thy imperfect knowledge will be detected at once,—this we should confidently affirm to be Spanish, wherever we met it. So also a traveller with any experience in the composition of Spanish sermons and Spanish ollas could make no mistake in respect of the following : *A sermon without Augustine is as a stew without bacon* ‡. Thus *Big and empty, like the Heidelberg tun* §, could have its home only in Germany ; that enormous vessel, known as the Heidelberg tun, constructed to contain nearly 300,000 flasks, having now stood empty for hundreds of years. As regards, too, the following, *Not every parish-priest can wear Dr. Luther's shoes* ||, we could be in no doubt

---

[* The Germans say, 'Wer nicht hören will muss fühlen ' (He that will not hear must feel).]

† En casa del Moro no hables algarabia.

‡ Sermon sin Agostino, olla sin tocino.

§ Gross und leer, wie das Heidelberger Fass.

|| Doctor Luther's Schuhe sind nicht allen Dorfpriestern gerecht.

to what people it appertains. And this, *The world is a carcase, and they who gather round it are dogs,* plainly proclaims itself as belonging to those Eastern lands, where the unowned dogs prowling about the streets of a city are the natural scavengers, that would assemble round a carcase thrown in the way. So too the form which our own proverb, *Man's extremity, God's opportunity,* or as we sometimes have it, *When need is highest, help is nighest* * assumes among the Jews, namely this, *When the tale of bricks is doubled, Moses comes* †, plainly roots itself in the early history of that nation, being an allusion to Exod. v. 9–19, and without a knowledge of that history would be unintelligible altogether. The same may be said of this : *We must creep into Ebal, and leap into Gerizim ;* in other words, we must be slow to curse, and swift to bless. (Deut. xxvii. 12, 13.)

But while it is thus with some, which are bound by the very conditions of their existence to a narrow and peculiar sphere, or at all events move more naturally and freely in it than elsewhere, there are others on the contrary which we meet all the world over. True cosmopolites, they seem to have travelled from land to land, and to have made themselves an home equally in all. The Greeks obtained them probably from the older East, and

[* In the thirteenth century ' Proverbs of Hendyng ' this appears as ' When the bale is hest, thenne is the bote nest,' l. 176 (Böddeker, *Altenglische Dichtungen,* p. 295). In Italian : Il male è la vigilia del bene (Ill is the eve of well) ; in Persian : ' When the defile is narrowest it begins to open out.' So our own : ' The darkest hour is that before the dawn,' ' When the night is darkest the day is nearest,' ' When things come to the worst they mend.']

† Cum duplicantur lateres, Moses venit.

again imparted them to the Romans ; and from these they have found their way into all the languages of the western world.

Much, I think, might be learned from knowing what those truths are, which are so felt to be true by all nations, that all have loved to possess them in these compendious forms, wherein they may pass readily from mouth to mouth : which, thus cast into some happy form, have commended themselves to almost all people, and have become a portion of the common stock of the world's wisdom, in every land making for themselves a recognition and an home. Such a proverb, for instance, is *Man proposes, God disposes* * ; one which I am inclined to believe that every nation in Europe possesses, so deeply upon all men is impressed the sense of Hamlet's words, if not the words themselves :

> There's a divinity that *shapes* our ends,
> *Rough-hew* them how we will.

Sometimes the proverb does not actually in so many words repeat itself in various tongues. We have indeed exactly the same *thought ;* but it takes an outward shape and embodiment, varying according to the various countries and periods in which it has been current : we have proverbs totally diverse from one another in their form and appearance, but which yet, when we look a little deeper into them, prove to be at heart one and the same,

---

* La gente pone, y Dios dispone.—Der Mensch denkt's, Gott lenkt's. [It occurs in Green's *Palamedes,* 1588, in George Herbert's *Jacula Prudentum,* and as ' Homo proponit sed Deus disponit,' in Thomas à Kempis, *Imitatio* (F. E. Hulme, *Proverb Lore,* p. 73).]

all these their differences being thus only, so to speak, variations of the same air. These are almost always an amusing, often an instructive, study; and to trace this likeness in difference has an interest lively enough. Thus the *forms* of the proverb, which brings out the absurdity of those reproving others for a defect or a sin, to whom the same cleaves in an equal or i· a greater degree, have sometimes no visible connexion at all, or the very slightest, with one another; yet for all this the proverb is at heart and essentially but one. We say in English : *The kiln calls the oven, 'Burnt house'* ;—the Italians : *The pan says to the pot 'Keep off, or you'll smutch me* * ' ;—the Spaniards : *The raven cried to the crow, 'Avaunt, blackamoor* † ' ; —the Germans : *One ass nicknames another, Long-ears* ‡ ;—while it must be owned there is a certain originality in the Catalan version of the proverb : *Death said to the man with his throat cut, 'How ugly you look.'* Under how rich a variety of forms does one and the same thought array itself here.

Let me quote another illustration of the same fact. We probably take for granted that *Coals to Newcastle* § is a thoroughly English expression of the absurdity of sending to a place that which

* La padella dice al pajuolo, Fatti in là, che tu mi tigni.
† Dijó la corneja al cuervo, Quítate allá, negro.
‡ Ein Esel schimpft den andern, Langohr.
[§ This proverb is found at least as early as 1614 (*Notes and Queries*, 8th S. ii. 484). Fuller has it in 1650, 'So far from being needless pains it may bring considerable profit to carry *Char-coals* to *New-castle*' (*Pisgah Sight*, p. 128). James Melvill in his *Diary*, 1583, has, 'Salt to Dysert or Colles to Newcastell' (p. 163, Wodrow Soc. ed.).]

already abounds there, water to the sea, faggots to the wood :—and English of course it is in the outward garment which it wears ; but in its innermost being it belongs to the whole world and to all times. Thus the Greeks said : *Owls to Athens* *, Attica abounding with these birds ; the Rabbis : *Enchantments to Egypt,* Egypt being of old esteemed the headquarters of all magic ; the Orientals : *Pepper to Hindostan ;* and in the middle ages they had this proverb : *Indulgences to Rome,* Rome being the centre and source of this spiritual traffic ; and these by no means exhaust the list.†

Let me adduce some other variations of the same descriptions, though not running through quite so many languages. Thus compare the German, *Who lets one sit on his shoulders, shall have him presently sit on his head* ‡, with the Italian, *If thou suffer a calf to be laid on thee, within a little they'll clap on the cow* §, and, again, with the Spanish,

---

* Γλαῦκας εἰς Ἀθήνας. [Lat. noctuas Athenas porto, Polydori Vergilii Proverbiorum Liber, 1511, fol. xxv.]

[† Other parallels are Lat. ' In silvam ligna ferre,' to carry logs to the wood (Horace, *Satires* i. 10, 34) ; Jewish, ' oil to Olivet ' ; Lat. ' crocum in Ciliciam ' ; Asiatic, ' blades to Damascus ' ; Scot. ' puddings to Tranent ' ; Dut. ' firs to Norway ' (A. Cheviot, *Proverbs of Scotland*, p. 73) ; ' Spaanderen naar Noorwegen brengen (Bellezza, *Proverbi Inglesi*, p. 49) ; ' Poma Alcinoo dare ' ; Ital. ' Vender il miele a chi ha le api ' (to sell honey to a beekeeper). Langland, *Piers Plowman*, B., xv. 332 (ab. 1370), has ' to woke Themese with water ' (to moisten the Thames with water), which later appears as ' to cast water into the Thames ' (or ' into the sea ') ; French, ' porter de l'eau à la rivière.']

‡ Wer sich auf der Achsel sitzen lässt, dem sitzt man nachher auf dem Kopfe.

§ Se ti lasci metter in spalla il vitello, quindi a poco ti metteran la vacca.

Give me where I may sit down ; I will make where I may lie down *. They all three plainly contain one and the same hint that undue liberties are best resisted at the outset, being otherwise liable to be followed up by other and greater ones ; but this under how rich and humorous a variety of forms. Not very different are these that follow. We say : *Daub yourself with honey, and you'll be covered with flies ;* the Danes : *Make yourself an ass, and you'll have every man's sack on your shoulders ;* while the French : *Who makes himself a sheep, the wolf devours him* † ; and the Persians : *Be not all sugar, or the world will gulp thee down* ‡ ; to which they add, however, as its necessary complement, *nor yet all wormwood, or the world will spit thee out.* Or again, we are content to say without a figure : *The receiver's as bad as the thief ;* but the French : *He sins as much who holds the sack, as he who puts into it* § ; and the Germans : *He who holds the ladder is as guilty as he who mounts the wall* ‖ . We say : *A stitch in time saves nine ;* the Spaniards : *Who repairs not his gutter, repairs his whole house* ¶. We say : *Misfortunes never come single ;* the Italians have no less than three proverbs to express the same popular conviction : *Blessed is that misfortune which comes single ;* and again : *One misfortune*

---

* Dame donde me asiente, que yo haré donde me acueste.

† Qui se fait brebis, le loup le mange.

‡ There is a Catalan proverb to the same effect : Qui de tot es moll, de tot es foll. [He who is soft in everything is a fool in everything.]

§ Autant pèche celui qui tient le sac, que celui qui met dedans.

‖ Wer die Leiter hält, ist so schuldig wie der Dieb.

¶ Quien no adoba gotera, adoba casa entera.

T.E.P.   F

is the vigil of another ; and again : *A misfortune
and a friar are seldom alone* *. Or once more, the
Russians say : *Call a peasant ' Brother ', he'll
demand to be called ' Father '* ; the Italians : *Reach
a peasant your finger, he'll grasp your fist* †. Many
languages have this proverb : *God gives the cold
according to the cloth* ‡ ; it is very beautiful, but
attains not to the tender beauty of our own : *God
tempers the wind to the shorn lamb.*§

And, as in that last example, so not seldom will
there be an evident superiority of a proverb in
one language over one, which however resembles it
closely, in another. Moving in the same sphere, it
will yet be richer, fuller, deeper. Thus our own,
A burnt child fears the fire,‖ is good ; but that of
many tongues, *A scalded dog fears cold water,* is
better still. Ours does but express that those who
have suffered once will henceforward be timid in
respect of that same thing from which they have
suffered ; but that other the tendency to exagger-

---

* Benedetto è quel male, che vien solo.—Un mal è la
vigilia dell' altro.—Un male ed un Frate di rado soli.
    † Al villano, se gli porgi il dito, ei prende la mano.
    ‡ Dieu donne le froid selon le drap.—Cada cual siente
el frio como anda vestido [Every one feels the cold
according as he is clad.—Spanish].
    [§ This proverb which is found in Sterne and occurs
also in French—' A brebis tondue Dieu mesure le vent '—
is a variant of Herbert's ' To a close-shorn sheep God
gives wind by measure ' (*Jacula Prudentum,* 1640).]
    [‖ That child with draweth is hond
        From the fur and the brond
        That hath byfore bue brend.
    ' Brend child fur dredeth,'
                Quoth Hendyng (1280, ll. 181–4).
    Portuguese, ' Gato escaldado d'aqua fria tem medo '
(The scalded cat is afraid of cold water). Compare ' Tran-
quillas etiam naufragus horret aquas " — Ovid ; see
F. E. Hulme, *Proverb Lore,* p. 72.]

ate such fears, so that now they shall fear even where no fear is. And the fact that so it will be, clothes itself in an almost infinite variety of forms. Thus one Italian proverb says : *A dog which has been beaten with a stick, is afraid of its shadow ;* and another, which could only have had its birth in the sunny South, where the glancing but harmless lizard so often darts across your path : *Whom a serpent has bitten a lizard alarms* *. With a little variation from this, the Jewish Rabbis had said long before : *One bitten by a serpent, is afraid of a rope's end ;* even that which bears so remote a resemblance to a serpent as this does, shall now inspire him with terror ; and the Cingalese, still expressing the same thought, but with imagery borrowed from their own tropic clime : *The man who has received a beating from a firebrand, runs away at sight of a firefly.*

Some of our Lord's sayings contain the same lessons which the proverbs of the Jewish Rabbis contained already ; for He was willing to bring forth even from His treasury things old as well as new ; but it is very instructive to observe how they acquire in His mouth a dignity and decorum which, it may be, they wanted before. We are all familiar with that word in the Sermon on the Mount, 'Whosoever shall compel thee to go a mile, go with him twain '. The Rabbis had a proverb to match, lively and piquant enough, but certainly lacking the gravity of this, and which never could have fallen from the same lips : *If thy neighbour call thee ass, put a packsaddle on thy back ;* do not, that is, withdraw thyself from the wrong, but rather

* Cui serpe mozzica, lucerta teme.

go forward to meet it. But thus, in least as in greatest, it was His to make all things new.

Sometimes a proverb, without changing its shape altogether, will yet on the lips of different nations be slightly modified ; and these modifications, slight as often they are, may not the less be eminently characteristic. Thus in English we say, *The river past, and God forgotten,* to express with how mournful a frequency He whose assistance was invoked, it may have been earnestly, in the moment of peril, is remembered no more, so soon as by His help the danger has been surmounted. The Spaniards have the proverb too ; but it is with them : *The river past, the saint forgotten* *, the saints being in Spain more prominent objects of invocation than God. And the Italian form of it sounds a still sadder depth of ingratitude : *The peril past, the saint mocked* † ; the vows made to him in peril remaining unperformed in safety ; and he treated something as, in Greek story, Juno was treated by Mandrabulus the Samian ; who, having under her auspices and through her direction discovered a gold mine, in his instant gratitude vowed to her a golden ram ; which he presently exchanged in intention for a silver one ; and again this for a very small brass one ; and this for nothing at all ; the rapidly descending scale of whose gratitude, with the entire disappearance of his thankoffering, might very profitably live in our memories, as so perhaps it would be less likely to repeat itself in our lives.

* El rio passado, el santo olvidado.
† Passato il punto, gabbato il santo.

THE POETRY, WIT, AND WISDOM OF PROVERBS

IT will be my endeavour in the three lectures which I have still to deliver to justify the attention which I have claimed on behalf of proverbs from you, not merely by appealing to the authority of others, who at different times have prized and made much of them, but by bringing out and setting before you, so far as I have the skill to do it, some of the merits and excellencies by which they are mainly distinguished. Their wit, their wisdom, their poetry, the delicacy, the fairness, the manliness which characterize so many of them, their morality, their theology, will all by turns come under our consideration. Yet shall I beware of presenting them to you as though they embodied these nobler qualities only. I shall not keep out of sight that there are proverbs, coarse, selfish, unjust, cowardly, profane ; ' maxims ' wholly undeserving of the honour implied by that name *. Still, as my pleasure, and I doubt not yours, is rather in the wheat than in the tares, I shall, while I do not conceal this, prefer to dwell in the main on the nobler features which they present.

* Regulæ quæ inter *maximas* numerari merentur.

And first, in regard of the poetry of proverbs—whatever is *from* the people, or truly *for* the people, whatever either springs from their bosom, or has been cordially accepted by them, still more whatever unites both these conditions, will have poetry, imagination, in it. For little as the people's craving after wholesome nutriment of the imaginative faculty, and after an entrance into a fairer and more harmonious world than that sordid and confused one with which often they are surrounded, is duly met and satisfied, still they yearn after all this with an honest hearty yearning, which must put to shame the palled indifference, the only affected enthusiasm of too many, whose opportunities of cultivating this glorious faculty have been so immeasurably greater than theirs. This being so, and proverbs being, as we have seen, the sayings that have found favour with the people, their peculiar inheritance, we may be quite sure that there will be poetry, imagination, passion, in them. So much we might affirm beforehand ; our closer examination of them will confirm the confidence which we have been bold to entertain.

Thus we may expect to find that they will contain often bold imagery, striking comparisons ; and such they do. Let serve as an example our own : *Gray hairs are death's blossoms* * ; or the Italian : *Time is an inaudible file* † ; or the Greek :

---

* In German : Grau' Haare sind Kirchhofsblumen. [Similarly in Greek an old man with hoary hair is said to be ' in blossom,' ἠνθισμένος (Sophocles, *Electra*, l. 43), according to one interpretation, and in Hebrew ' The almond tree is in flower ' describes the silvery locks of old age (Eccles. xii. 5, see Delitzsch, *in loco*).]

† Il tempo è una lima sorda.

Man a bubble *; which Jeremy Taylor has expanded into such glorious poetry in the opening of the *Holy Dying ;* or that Turkish : *Death is a black camel which kneels at every man's gate ;* to take up, that is, the burden of a coffin there ; or this Arabic one, on the never satisfied eye of desire : *Nothing but a handful of dust will fill the eye of man ;* or another from the same quarter, worthy of Mecca's prophet himself, and of the earnestness with which he realized Gehenna, whatever else he may have come short in : *There are no fans in hell ;* or this other, also from the East : *Hold all skirts of thy mantle extended, when heaven is raining gold ;* improve, that is, to the uttermost the happier crises of thy spiritual life ; or this Indian, to the effect that good should be returned for evil : *The sandal tree perfumes the axe that fells it ;* or this one, current in the Middle Ages : *Whose life lightens, his words thunder* † ; or once more, this Chinese : *Towers are measured by their shadows, and great men by their calumniators* ‡ *;* however this last may have somewhat of an artificial air as tried by our standard of the proverb.

There may be poetry in a play upon words ; and such we shall hardly fail to acknowledge in that beautiful Spanish proverb : *La verdad es siempre verde,* which I must leave in its original

---

* Πομφόλυξ ὁ ἄνθρωπος.
[Compare Sir H. Wotton's—
' The world's a bubble : and the life of man less than a span '
        Reliquiæ Wottonianæ, 1672, p. 397).]

† Cujus vita fulgor, ejus verba tonitrua. Cf. Mark iii.
17 : υἱοὶ βροντῆς.

[‡ ' Never yet was noble man but made ignoble talk.'—
Tennyson, *Elaine,* l. 1082.]

form ; for were I to translate it, *The truth is always green,* its charm and chief beauty would be looked for in vain.   It finds its pendant and complement in another, which I must also despair of adequately rendering :   *Gloria vana florece, y no grana ;* which would express this truth, namely, that vain glory can shoot up into stalk and ear, but can never attain to the full grain in the ear.   Nor can we, I think, refuse the title of poetry to this Eastern proverb, in which the wish that a woman may triumph over her enemies, clothes itself thus : *May her enemies stumble over her hair ;*—may she flourish so, may her hair, the outward sign of this prosperity, grow so rich and long, may it so sweep the ground, that her detractors and persecutors may be entangled by it and fall.

And then, how exquisitely witty many proverbs are.   Thus, not to speak of one familiar to us all, which is perhaps the queen of all proverbs : *The road to hell is paved with good intentions* * ;   take this Scotch one : *A man may love his house well, without riding on the ridge* † ;   it is enough for a wise man to know what is precious to himself, without making himself ridiculous by evermore proclaiming it to the world ;   or this of our own : *When the devil is dead, he never wants a chief mourner ;* in other words, there is no abuse so enormous, no evil so flagrant, but that the interests

* Admirably glossed in the *Guesses at Truth :* ' Pluck up the stones, ye sluggards, and break the devil's head with them.'

[† This proverb is given in Camden, *Remaines Concerning Britaine,* 1637, p. 291.]

or passions of some will be so bound up in its continuance that they will lament its extinction;
or this Italian : *When rogues go in procession, the
devil holds the cross* * ; when evil men have it thus
far their own way, then worst is best, and in the
inverted hierarchy which is then set up, the foremost in badness is foremost also in such honour as
is going.   Or consider how happily the selfishness
and bye-ends which too often preside at men's very
prayers are noted in this Portuguese : *Cobblers
go to mass, and pray that cows may die* † ; that is,
that so leather may be cheap.   Or, take another,
a German one, noting with slightest exaggeration
a measure of charity which is only too common :
*He will swallow an egg, and give away the shells
in alms;* or this from the Talmud, of which I
will leave the interpretation to yourselves : *All
kinds of wood burn silently, except thorns, which
crackle and call out, We too are wood.*

The wit of proverbs spares few or none.   They
are, as may be supposed, especially intolerant of
fools.   *We* say : *Fools grow without watering;* no
need therefore of adulation or flattery, to quicken
them to a ranker growth ; for indeed *The more you
stroke the cat's tail, the more he raises his back* ‡ ; and
the Russians : *Fools are not planted or sowed,
they grow of themselves;* while the Spaniards : *If
folly were a pain, there would be crying in every*

---

* Quando i furbi vanno in processione, il diavolo
porta la croce.

† Vaô á missa çapateiros, rogaô a Deos que morraô os
carneiros.

‡ This is Swedish : Zu mera man stryken Katten pá
Swanzen, zu mera pyser pan.

house * ; having further an exquisitely witty one
on learned folly as the most intolerable of all
follies : *A fool, unless he know Latin, is never a
great fool* †. And here is excellently unfolded to
us the secret of the fool's confidence : *Who knows
nothing, doubts nothing* ‡.

The shafts of their pointed satire are directed
with an admirable impartiality against men of
every degree, so that none of us will be found to
have wholly escaped. To pass over those, and
they are exceedingly numerous, which are aimed
at members of the monastic orders §, I must fain
hope that this Bohemian one, pointing at the
clergy, is not true ; for it certainly argues no very
forgiving temper on our parts in cases where we
have been, or fancy ourselves to have been, wronged.
It is as follows : *If you have offended a clerk, kill
him ; else you never will have peace with him* ‖.
And another proverb, worthy to take its place

---

* Si la locura fuese dolores, en cada casa darian voces.

† Tonto, sin saber latin, nunca es gran tonto. [Compare :—' He that is vaine and foolish of himselfe, becomes more so by the addition of learning '—*Crumms Fal'n from King James's Table* (*Overbury's Works*, ed. Rimbault, p. 269). ' A scholar . . . if he has a wrong judgment and an ill taste . . . grows every day either a more insufferable pedant or distinguished coxcomb.'—Eustace Budgell].

‡ Qui rien ne sçait, de rien ne doute.

§ An earnest preacher of righteousness just before the Reformation quotes this one as current about them : Quod agere veretur obstinatus diabolus, intrepide agit reprobus et contumax monachus [What an inveterate devil would be afraid to do a wicked and contumacious monk does without fear].

‖ It is Huss who, denouncing the sins of the clergy of his day, has preserved this proverb for us : Malum proverbium contra nos confinxerunt, dicentes, Si offenderis clericum, interfice eum ; alias nunquam habebis pacem cum illo.

among the best even of the Spanish, charges the clergy with being the authors of the chiefest spiritual mischiefs which have risen up in the Church : *By the vicar's skirts the devil climbs up into the belfry* *. Nor do physicians appear in the Middle Ages to have been in very high reputation for piety ; for a Latin medieval proverb boldly proclaims : *Where there are three physicians, there are two atheists* †. And as for lawyers, this of the same period, *Legista, nequista* ‡, expresses itself not with such brevity only, but with such downright plainness of speech, that I shall excuse myself from attempting to render it into English. Nor do other sorts and conditions of men escape. ' The miller tolling with his golden thumb ' has been often the object of malicious insinuations ; and of him the German have a proverb : *What is bolder than a miller's neckcloth, which takes a thief by the throat every morning* § ? Evenhanded justice might perhaps require that I should find caps for other heads ; and it is not that such are wanting, nor yet out of fear lest any should be offended, but only because I must needs hasten onward, that

* Por las haldas del vicario sube el diablo al campanario.

† Ubi tres Medici, duo Athei [Referred to in the opening sentence of Sir Thos. Browne's *Religio Medici*, 1643, and Sir Kenelm Digby's note thereon]. Of course those which imply that they shorten rather than prolong the term of life, are numerous, as for instance, the old French : Qui court après le mière, court après la bière. [He who runs after the doctor runs after his coffin.]

‡ In German : Juristen, bösen Christen [Lawyers bad Christians].

§ Bebel : Dicitur in proverbio nostro ; nihil esse audacius indusio molitoris, cum omni tempore matutino furem collo apprehendat.

I leave this part of my subject without further development.

What a fine knowledge of the human heart will they often display. I know not whether this Persian saying on the subtleties of pride is a proverb in the very strictest sense of the word, but it is forcibly uttered : *Thou shalt sooner detect an ant moving in the dark night on the black earth, than all the motions of pride in thine heart.* And on the wide reach of this sin the Italians say : *If pride were an art, how many graduates we should have* *; and how excellent and searching is this word of theirs on the infinitely various shapes which this protean sin will assume : *There are who despise pride with a greater pride* †, one which might almost seem to have been founded on the story of Diogenes, who, treading under his feet a rich carpet of Plato's, exclaimed ' Thus I trample on the ostentation of Plato ' ; ' With an ostentation of thine own,' was the other's excellent retort ; —even as on another occasion he observed, with admirable wit, that he saw the pride of the Cynic peeping through the rents of his mantle : for indeed pride can array itself quite as easily in rags as in purple ; can affect squalors as earnestly as splendours ; the lowest place and the last is of itself no security at all for humility ; and out of a sense of this *we* very well have said : *As proud go behind as before.*

Sometimes in their subtle observation of life, they arrive at conclusions which we would very willingly question or reject, but to which it is

---

* Se la superbia fosse arte, quanti Dottori avressimo.
† Tal sprezza la superbia con una maggior superbia.

^{i}mpossible to refuse a certain amount of assent. Thus it is with the very striking German proverb : *One foe is too many ; and an hundred friends too few* *. There speaks out in this a sense of how much more *active* a principle in this world will hate be sometimes than love.   The hundred friends will *wish* you well ; but the one foe will *do* you ill.   Their benevolence will be ordinarily passive ; his malevolence will be constantly active ; it will be *animosity*, or spiritedness in evil.   The proverb will have its use, if we are stirred up by it to prove its assertion false, to show that, in very many cases at least, there is no such blot as it would set on the scutcheon of true friendship.   In the same rank of unwelcome proverbs I must range this Persian one : *Of four things every man has more than he knows ; of sins, of debts, of years, and of foes ;* and this Spanish : *One father can support ten children ; ten children cannot support one father ;* which, in so far as it rests upon a certain ground of truth, suggests a painful reflection in regard of the less strength which there must be in the filial than in the paternal affection, since to the one those acts of self-sacrificing love are easy, which to the other are hard, and often impossible.   But yet, seeing that it is the order of God's providence in the world that fathers should in all cases support children, while it is the exception when children are called to support parents, one can only admire that wisdom which has made the instincts of natural affection to run rather in the descending than in the ascending line ; a wisdom to which this pro-

---

* Ein Feind ist zu viel ; und hundert Freunde sind zu wenig.

verb, though with a certain exaggeration of the facts, bears witness.

How exquisitely delicate is the touch of this French proverb : *It is easy to go afoot, when one leads one's horse by the bridle* *. How fine and subtle an insight into the inner workings of the human heart is here ; how many cheap humilities are here set at their true worth. It *is* easy to stoop from state, when that state may be resumed at will ; easy for one to part with luxuries and indulgences, which he only parts with exactly so long as it may please himself. No reason indeed is to be found in this comparative easiness for the not ' going afoot ' ; on the contrary, it may be to him a most profitable exercise ; but every reason for not esteeming the doing so too highly, nor setting it on a level with the trudging upon foot of him, who has no horse to fall back on at whatever moment he may please.

There is, and always must be, some rough work to be done in the world ; work which, though rough, is not therefore in the least ignoble ; and the schemes, so daintily conceived, of a luxurious society, which repose on a tacit assumption that nobody shall have to do this work, are touched with a fine irony in this Arabic proverb : *If I am master, and thou art master, who shall drive the asses* † ?

Again, how clever is the satire of the following

---

* Il est aisé d'aller à pied, quand on tient son cheval par la bride.

† The Gallegan proverb, *You a lady, I a lady, who shall drive the hogs a-field ?* (Vos dona, yo dona, quen botara a porca fora ?) is only a variation of this.

Haytian proverb, which, however, I must introduce
with a little preliminary explanation. It was one
current among the slave population of St. Domingo,
and with it they ridiculed the ambition and pre-
tension of the mulatto race immediately above
them. These, in imitation of the French planters,
must have their duels too—duels, however, which
had nothing earnest or serious about them, in-
variably ending in a reconciliation and a feast,
the kids which furnished the latter being in fact
the only sufferers, their blood that which alone was
shed. All this the proverb uttered : *Mulattoes
fight, kids die* *.

And proverbs, witty in themselves, often become
wittier still in their application, like gems that
acquire new brilliancy from their setting, or from
some novel light in which they are held. No
writer that I know of has an happier skill in thus
adding wit to the witty than Fuller, the Church
historian. Let me confirm this assertion by one
or two examples drawn from his writings. He is
describing the indignation, the outcries, the remon-
strances, which the thousandfold extortions, the
intolerable exactions of the Papal See gave birth
to in England during the reigns of such subservient
kings as our Third Henry ; yet he will not have
his readers to suppose that the Popes fared a whit
the worse for all this outcry which was raised
against them ; not so, for *The fox thrives best when
he is most cursed* † ; the very loudness of the

---

* Mulates qua battent, cabrites qua morts.

† A proverb of many tongues beside our own : thus in
the Italian : Quanto più la volpe è maladetta, tanto
maggior preda fa.

clamour was itself rather an evidence how well they were faring. Or again, he is telling of that Duke of Buckingham, well known to us through Shakespeare's *Richard the Third*, who, having helped the tyrant to a throne, afterwards took mortal displeasure against him ; this displeasure he sought to hide, till a season arrived for showing it with effect, in the deep of his heart, but in vain ; for, as Fuller observes, *It is hard to halt before a cripple ;* the arch-hypocrite Richard, he to whom dissembling was as a second nature, saw through and detected at once the shallow Buckingham's clumsier deceit. And the *Church History* abounds with similar happy applications. Fuller, indeed, possesses so much of the wit out of which proverbs spring, that it is not seldom difficult to tell whether he is adducing a proverb, or uttering some proverb-like saying of his own. Thus, I cannot remember ever to have met any of the following, which yet sound like proverbs—the first on solitude as preferable to ill fellowship : *Better ride alone than have a thief's company* * ; the second against certain who disparaged one whose excellencies they would have found it very difficult to imitate : *They who complain that Grantham steeple stands awry, will not set a straighter by it* †, and in this he warns against despising in any the tokens of honourable toil : *Mock not a cobbler for his black thumbs* ‡.

But the glory of proverbs, that, perhaps, which strikes us most often and most forcibly in regard of them is their shrewd common sense, the sound wis-

* *Holy State,* b. 3, c. 5.
† B. 2, c. 23.
‡ B. 3, c. 2.

dom for the management of our own lives, and of our intercourse with our fellows, which so many of them contain. In truth, there is no region of practical life which they do not occupy, for which they do not supply some wise hints and counsels and warnings. There is hardly a mistake which in the course of our lives we have committed, but some proverb, had we known and attended to its lesson, might have saved us from it. ' Adages ', indeed, according to the more probable etymology of that word, they are, *apt for action* and use *.

Thus, how many of these popular sayings and what good ones there are on the wisdom of governing the tongue—I speak not now of those urging the *duty*, though such are by no means wanting—but the wisdom, prudence, and profit of knowing how to keep silence as well as how to speak. The Persian, perhaps, is familiar to many : *Speech is silvern, silence is golden ;* with which we may compare the Italian : *Who speaks, sows ; who keeps silence, reaps* † *;* and on the *safety* that is in silence, I know none happier than another from the same quarter, and one most truly characteristic of Italian caution : *Silence was never written down* ‡ ; while on the other hand, we are excellently warned of the irrevocableness of the word which has once gone from us in this Eastern proverb : *Of thine unspoken word thou art master : thy spoken word is master of*

---

* Adagia, ad agendum apta ; this is the etymology of the word given by Festus.   [The latter part of the word is rather from *agio* = *ajo*, I say.]

† Chi parla semina, chi tace raccoglie ; compare the Swedish : Bättre tyga än illa tala (Better silence than ill speech).

‡ Il tacer non fù mai scritto.

T.E.P.   G

thee * ; even as the same is set out elsewhere by
many striking comparisons ; it is the arrow from
the bow, the stone from the sling ;   and, once
launched, can as little be recalled as these †.   Our
own, *He who says what he likes, shall hear what he
does not like,* gives a further motive for self-govern-
ment in speech ;   while this Spanish is in an higher
strain : *The evil which issues from thy mouth falls
into thy bosom* ‡.   Nor is it enough to abstain ourselves from all such words ;   we must not make
ourselves partakers in those of others ;   which it is
only too easy to do ;   for, as the Chinese have said
very well : *He who laughs at an impertinence,
makes himself its accomplice.*

And then, in proverbs not a few what profitable
warnings have we against the fruits of evil companionship, as in that homely one of our own :
He that lies down with dogs shall rise up with fleas § ;
or, again, in the old Hebrew one : *Two dry sticks
will set on fire one green ;* or, in another from the
East, which has to do with the same theme, and
plainly shows whither such companionship will
lead : *He that takes the raven for a guide, shall light
upon carrion.*

* [Closely similar is this from Quarles : ' A word unspoken is, like the sword in thy scabbard, thine ; if vented
thy sword is in another's hand.''—*Enchridion,* 1641,
cent. 3, xxxii.]

† Palabra de boca, piedra de honda.—Palabra y piedra
suelta no tiene vuelta [A word from the mouth is a
stone from a sling.—A word and a stone when discharged
never come back again].

‡ El mal que da tu boca sale, en tu seno se cae.

§ Quien con perros se echa, con pulgas se levanta.
[This proverb has been traced up to Seneca : ' Qui
cum canibus concumbunt cum pulicibus surgent.'   See
F. E. Hulme, *Proverb Lore,* p. 19.]

What warnings do many contain against unreasonable expectations, against a looking for perfection in a world of imperfection, and generally a demanding of more from life than life can yield. *We* note very well the folly of one addicted to this, saying : *He expects better bread than can be made of wheat :* and the Portuguese : *He that will have an horse without fault, let him go afoot ;* and the French : *Where the goat is tied, there she must browse* *. Again, what a good word of caution in respect of the wisdom of considering oftentimes a step which, being once taken, is taken for ever, lies in the following Russian proverb : *Measure thy cloth ten times : thou canst cut it but once.* And in this Spanish the final issues of procrastination are well set forth : *By the street of ' By-and-bye ' one arrives at the house of ' Never '* †. In how pleasant a way discretion in avoiding all appearance of evil is urged in the following Chinese : *In a field of melons tie not thy shoe ; under a plum tree adjust not thy cap.* And this Danish warns us well against relying too much on other men's silence, since there is no rarer gift than the capacity of keeping a secret : *Tell nothing to thy friend which thine enemy may not know.* Here is a word which we owe to Italy, and which, laid to heart, might keep men out of law-suits, or, being in them, from refusing to accept tolerable terms of accommodation : *The robes of lawyers are lined with the obstinacy of suitors*‡. Other words of wisdom and warning,

---

* La ou la chèvre est attachée, il faut qu'elle broute.
† Por la calle de despues se va à la casa de nunca.
‡ Le vesti degl' avvocati sono fodrate dell' ostinazion dei litiganti.

for so I must esteem them, are these ; this, on the danger of being overset by prosperity : *Every-thing may be borne, except good fortune* * ; with which may be compared our own : *Bear wealth, poverty will bear itself ;* and another Italian which says : *In prosperity no altars smoke* †. This is on the disgrace which will sooner or later follow upon dressing ourselves out in intellectual finery that does not belong to us : *Who arrays himself in other men's garments, is stripped in the middle of the street* ‡ ; he is detected and laid bare when and where detection is most shameful.

Of the same miscellaneous character, and de-rived from quarters the most diverse, but all of them of an excellent sense or shrewdness, are the following. This is from Italy : *Who sees not the bottom, let him not pass the water* §. This is current among the free blacks of Hayti : *Before fording the river, do not curse Mrs. Alligator* ‖ : provoke not wantonly those in whose power you presently may be. This is Spanish : *Call me not ' olive ', till you see me gathered* ¶ ; being nearly parallel to our own : *Praise a fair day at night ;* and this French : *Take the first advice of a woman, and not the second* ** ; a proverb of much wisdom ; for in

---

* Ogni cosa si sopporta, eccetto il buon tempo.

† Nella prosperità non fumano gli altari.

‡ Quien con ropa agena se viste, en la calle se queda encueros.

§ Chi non vede il fondo, non passi l'acqua.

‖ Avant traversé rivier, pas juré maman caiman. This and one or two other Haytian proverbs quoted in this volume I have derived from a curious article, *Les mœurs et la littérature nègres*, by Gustave D'Alaux, in the *Revue des deux Mondes*, Mai 15me, 1852.

¶ No me digas oliva, hasta que me veas cogida.

**Prends le premier conseil d'une femme, et non le second.

processes of reasoning, out of which the second counsels would spring, women may and will be, inferior to us ; but in intuitions, in moral intuitions above all, they surpass us far ; they have what Montaigne ascribes to them in a remarkable word, ' l'esprit *primesautier* ', the leopard's spring, which takes its prey, if it take it at all, at the first bound.

And I cannot but think that for as many as are seeking diligently to improve their time and opportunities of knowledge, with at the same time little of either which they can call their own, a very useful hint and warning against an error which lies very near, is contained in the little Latin proverb : *Compendia, dispendia.* Nor indeed for them only, but for all, and in numberless respects it often proves true that a short cut may be a very long way home ; yet the proverb can never be applied better than to those little catechisms of science, those skeleton outlines of history, those epitomes of all useful information, those thousand delusive short cuts to the attainment of that knowledge, which can indeed only be acquired by them that are content to travel on the king's highway, on the old, and as I must still call it, the royal road of patience, perseverance, and toil. Surely these *compendia*, so meagre and so hungry, with little food for the intellect, with less for the affections, we may style with fullest right *dispendia*, wasteful as they generally prove of whatever time and labour and money is bestowed upon them ; and every wise man will set his seal to this word, as wisely as it is grandly spoken : ' All spacious minds, attended with the felicities of means and leisure, will fly abridgements as bane.'

And being on the subject of books and the choice of books, let me put before you a proverb, and in this reading age a very serious one ; it comes to us from Italy, and it says : *There is no worse robber than a bad book* *. Indeed, none worse, nor so bad ; other robbers may spoil us of our money ; but this robber of our ' goods '—of our time at any rate, even assuming the book to be only negatively bad ; but of how much more, of our principles, our faith, our purity of heart, supposing its badness to be positive, and not negative only. And one more on books may fitly find place here : *Dead men open living men's eyes* † ; at least I take it to be such ; and to contain implicitly the praise of history, and an announcement of the instruction which it will yield us ‡.

Here are one or two prudent words on education. *A child may have too much of its mother's blessing ;* yes, for that *blessing* may be no blessing, but rather a curse, if it take the shape of foolish and fond indulgence ; and in the same strain is this German :

* Non v' è il peggior ladro d un cattivo libro.
[† Compare Bacon's remark : ' Optimi consiliarii mortui, Books will speake plaine when counsellors blanch.' —*Essays*, p. 327 (ed. Arber). ' Alonzo of Arragon was wont to say of himselfe " that he was a great Necromancer, for that he used to aske counsell of the dead." '— *Apophth.* 105 (ed. 1625).
    ' There studious let me sit
And hold high converse with the mighty dead.'
                                        Thomson.
    ' My days among the dead are passed . . .
    My never-failing friends are they
    With whom I converse day by day.'
                                        Southey.
‡ Los muertos abren los ojos á los vivos.

Better the child weep than the father *. And this, like many others, is found in so many tongues, that it cannot be ascribed to one rather than another : *More springs in the garden than the gardener ever sowed* †. It is a proverb for many, but most of all for parents and teachers, that they lap not themselves in a false dream of security, as though nothing was at work or growing in the minds of the young in their guardianship, but what they themselves had sown there, as though there was not another who might very well have sown his tares beside and among any good seed of their sowing. At the same time the proverb has also its happier side. There may be, there often are, better things also in this garden than ever the earthly gardener set there, seeds of the more immediate sowing of God. In either of its aspects this proverb is one deserving to be laid to heart.

Proverbs will sometimes outrun and implicitly anticipate conclusions, which are only after long struggles and efforts arrived at as the formal and undoubted conviction of all thoughtful men. After how long a conflict has that been established as a maxim in political economy, which the brief Italian proverb long ago announced : *Gold's worth is gold* ‡. What millions upon millions of national wealth have been as much lost as if they had been thrown into the sea, from the inability of those who have had the destinies of nations in

---

* Es ist besser das Kind weine denn der Vater.
† Nace en la huerta lo que no siembra el hortelano.
‡ Oro è, che oro vale ;—and of the multitudes that are rushing to the Australian gold-fields, some may find this also true : Più vale guadagnar in loto che perder in oro.

their hands to grasp this simple proposition, that everything which could purchase money, or which money would fain purchase, was as really wealth as the money itself. What forcing of national industries into unnatural channels has resulted from this, what mischievous restrictions in the buying and selling of one people with another. Nay, can the truth which this proverb affirms be said even now to be accepted without gainsaying—so long as the talk about the balance of trade being in favour of or against a nation, as the fear of draining a country of its gold, still survive ?

Here is a proverb of many tongues : *One sword keeps another in its scabbard* * ; —surely a far wiser and far manlier word than the puling yet mischievous babble of our shallow Peace Societies, which, while they fancy that they embody, and they only embody, the true spirit of Christianity, proclaim themselves in fact ignorant of all which it teaches ; for they dream of having peace the fruit, while at the same time the root of bitterness out of which have grown all the wars and fightings that have ever been in the world, namely the lusts which stir in men's members, remain strong and vigorous as ever. But no ; it is not they that are the peacemakers : in the face of an evil world, and of a world determined to continue in its evil, *He who bears the sword,* and though he fain would not, yet knows how, if need be, to wield it, *he bears peace* †.

One of the most remarkable features of a good proverb is the singular variety of applications

* Una spada tien l' altra nel fodro.
† Qui porte épée, porte paix.

which it will admit, which indeed it challenges and invites. Not lying on the surface of things, but going deep down to their heart, it will be found capable of being applied again and again, under circumstances the most different ; like the gift of which Solomon spake, ' whithersoever it turneth, it prospereth ' ; or like a diamond cut and polished upon many sides, which reflects and refracts the light upon every one. There can be no greater mistake than the attempt to tie it down and restrict it to a single application, when indeed the very character of it is that it is ever finding or making new ones for itself.

It is nothing strange that with words of Eternal Wisdom this should be so, and in respect of them my assertion cannot need a proof. I will, notwithstanding, adduce as a first confirmation of it a scriptural proverb, one which fell from the Lord's lips in his last prophecies about Jerusalem : *Wheresoever the carcase is, there will the eagles be gathered together* (Matt. xxiv. 28) ; and which probably He had taken up from Job (xxxix. 30). Who would venture to say that He had exhausted the meaning of this wonderful saying ? For is it not properly inexhaustible ? All history is a comment on these words. Wherever there is a Church or a people abandoned by the spirit of life, and so a carcase, tainting the atmosphere of God's moral world, around it assemble the ministers and messengers of Divine justice, ' the eagles ' (or vultures more strictly, for the true eagle does not feed on aught but what itself has slain), the scavengers of God's moral world ; scenting out as by a mysterious instinct the prey from afar, and charged to remove presently the offence out of the way.   This proverb, for the saying has passed upon the lips of men, and thus has become such, is being fulfilled evermore. The wicked Canaanites were the carcase, when the children of Israel entered into their land, the commissioned eagles that should remove them out of sight.   At a later day the Jews were themselves the carcase, and the Romans the eagles ; and when in the progress of decay, the Roman empire had quite lost the spirit of life, and those virtues of the family and the nation which had deservedly made it great, the northern tribes, the eagles now, came down upon it, to tear it limb from limb, and make room for a new creation that should grow up in its stead.   Again, the Persian empire was the carcase ; Alexander and his Macedonian hosts, the eagles that by unerring instinct gathered round it to complete its doom.   The Greek Church in the seventh century was too nearly a carcase to escape the destiny of such, and the armies of Islam scented their prey, and divided it among them.   In modern times Poland was, I fear, such a carcase ; and this one may affirm without in the least extenuating their guilt who partitioned it ; for it might have been just for it to suffer, what yet it was most unrighteous for others to inflict.   Nay, where do you not find an illustration of this proverb, from such instances on the largest scale as these, down to that of the silly and profligate heir, surrounded by sharpers and black-legs, and preyed on by these ? Everywhere it is true that *Wheresoever the carcase is, there will the eagles be gathered together.*

Or, again, consider such a proverb as the short but well-known one : *Extremes meet.*   Short as it

is, it is yet a motto on which whole volumes might
be written, which is finding its illustration every
day—in small and in great—in things trivial and
in things most important—in the histories of single
men, and in those of nations and of Churches.
Consider some of its every-day fulfilments—old
age ending in second childhood—cold performing
the effects of heat, and scorching as heat would
have done—the extremities alike of joy and of
grief finding utterance in tears—that which is
above all value declared to have no value at all, to
be 'invaluable'—the second singular 'thou'
instead of the plural 'you', employed in so many
languages to inferiors and to God, never to equals ;
just as servants and children are alike called by the
Christian name, but not those who stand in the
midway of intimacy between them. Or to take
some further illustrations from the moral world,
of extremes meeting ; observe how often those who
begin their lives as spendthrifts end them as misers ;
how often the flatterer and the calumniator meet
in the same person : out of a sense of which the
Italians say well : *Who paints me before, blackens me
behind* * ; observe how those who yesterday would
have sacrificed to Paul as a god, will to-day stone
him as a malefactor (Acts xiv. 18, 19 ; cf. xxviii.
4-6) ; even as Roman emperors would one day

* Chi dinanzi mi pinge, di dietro mi tinge. The history
of the word 'sycophant,' and the manner in which it has
travelled from its original to its present meaning, is a very
striking confirmation of this proverb's truth. [Compare
the German : 'Schmeichler sind Katzen, die vorne
lecken und hinten kratzen.' 'The amiable King had a
trick of giving a sly scratch with one hand while patting
and stroking with the other' (Macaulay, *Essay on Fred-
erick the Great*).]

have blasphemous honours paid to them by the
populace, and the next their bodies would be
dragged by a hook through the streets of the city,
to be flung into the common sewer. Or note again
in what close alliance hardness and softness, cruelty
and self-indulgence ('lust hard by hate'), are
continually found ; or in law, how the *summum
jus*, where unredressed by equity, becomes the
summa injuria, as in the case of Shylock's pound
of flesh, which was indeed no more than was in the
bond. Or observe on a greater scale, as lately in
France, how a wild and lawless democracy may be
transformed by the base trick of a conjuror into an
atrocious military tyranny *. Or read thought-
fully the history of the Church and of the sects, and
you will not fail to note what things apparently
the most remote are yet in the most fearful prox-
imity with one another : how often, for example, a
false asceticism has issued in frantic outbreaks of
fleshly lusts, and those who avowed themselves at
one time ambitious to live lives above men, have
ended in living lives below beasts. Again, take
note of England at the Restoration exchanging all
in a moment the sour strictness of the Puritans for
a licence and debauchery unknown to it before.
Or, once more, consider the exactly similar position
in respect of Scripture, taken up by the Romanists
on the one side, the Quakers and Familists on the
other. Seeming, and in much being, so remote
from one another, they yet have this fundamental
in common, that Scripture, insufficient in itself,

* How and why it is that extremes here meet, and what
are the inner affinities between a democracy and a tyranny,
Plato has wonderfully traced, *Rep.* ii. p. 217.

needs a supplement from without, those finding it in a Pope, and these in the ' inward light ' *.
With these examples before you, not to speak of the many others which might be adduced †, you will own, I think, that this proverb, *Extremes meet,* or its parallel, *Too far East is West,* reaches very far into the heart of things ; and with this for the present I must conclude.

---

* See Jeremy Taylor's *Dissuasive from Popery,* part 2 b. i. sect. ii, § 6.

† ' *Extremes meet.* Truths, of all others the most awful and interesting, are too often considered as *so* true, that they lose all the power of truths, and lie bedridden in the dormitory of the soul, side by side with the most despised and exploded errors.'—Coleridge, *Aids to Reflection.*

THE MORALITY OF PROVERBS

THE morality of proverbs is a subject which I
have not been able to leave wholly untouched
until now, for of necessity it has offered itself to
us continually, in one shape or another ; yet hitherto I have not regularly dealt with or considered
it. To it I propose to devote the present lecture.
But how, it may be asked at the outset, can any
general verdict be pronounced about them ? In
a family like theirs, spread so widely over the face
of the earth, must there not be found worthy
members and unworthy, proverbs noble and
base, holy and profane, heavenly and earthly ;—
yea, heavenly, earthly, and devilish ? What
common judgment of praise or censure can be
pronounced upon all of these ? Evidently none.
The only question, therefore, for our consideration must be, whether there exists any such large
and unquestionable preponderance either of the
better sort or of the worse, as shall give us a right
to pronounce a judgment on the whole in their
favour or against them, to affirm of them that their
preponderating influence and weight is thrown into
the balance of the good or of the evil.

And here I am persuaded that no one can have
devoted any serious attention to this aspect of

the subject, but will own (and seeing how greatly popular morals are affected by popular proverbs, will own with thankfulness) that, if not without serious exceptions, yet still in the main they range themselves under the banners of the right and of the truth ; he will allow that of so many as move in an ethical sphere at all, very far more are children of light and the day than of darkness and night. Indeed, the comparative paucity of unworthy proverbs is a very noticeable fact, and one to the causes of which I shall have presently to recur.

At the same time, when I affirm this, I find it necessary to make certain explanations, to draw certain distinctions. In the first place, I would not, by what I have said, in the least deny that an ample number of coarse proverbs are extant : it needs but to turn over a page or two of Ray's *Collection of English Proverbs*, or of Howell's, or indeed of any collection in any tongue, which has not been weeded carefully, to convince oneself of the fact ;—nor yet would I deny, that of these many may, more or less, live upon the lips of men. Having their birth, for the most part, in a period of a nation's literature and life, when men are much more plain-spoken, and have far fewer reticences than is afterwards the case, it is nothing strange that some of them, employing words forbidden now, but not forbidden then, should sound coarse and indelicate enough in our ears : while indeed there are others, whose offence and grossness these considerations, while they may mitigate, are quite insufficient to excuse. But at the same time, gross words and images (I speak not of wanton ones) bad as they may be, are altogether different from immoral maxims and rules of life. And it is these immoral maxims, unrighteous, selfish, or otherwise unworthy rules, of which I would affirm the number to be, if not absolutely, yet relatively small.

And then further, in estimating the morality of proverbs, this also will claim in justice not to be forgotten. In the same manner as coarse proverbs are not necessarily immoral, so the application which is made of a proverb by us may very often be hardhearted and selfish, while yet the proverb itself is very far from so being. This selfishness and hardness lay not in it of primary intention, but only by our abuse ; and in the cases of several, these two things, the proverb itself, and the ordinary employment of it, will demand to be kept carefully apart from one another. For instance : *He has made his bed, and now he must lie on it ; —As he has brewed, so he must drink ;—As he has sown, so must he reap* * ;—if these are employed to justify us in refusing to save others, so far as we may, from the consequences of their own folly, or imprudence, or even guilt, why then one can only say that they are very ill employed ; and there are few of us with whom it would not have gone hardly, had all those about us acted in the spirit of these

---

* They have for their Latin equivalents such as these : Colo quod aptâsti, ipsi tibi nendum est.—Qui vinum bibit, fæcem bibat.—Ut sementem feceris, ita metes. [What you have put on the distaff you must spin yourself.—Who drinks the wine must drink the dregs.—As thou hast sown so shalt thou reap. Compare δράσαντι παθέιν—Aesch. *Choeph.* 310 (The doer must suffer) ; in Italian, ' chi la fa l' aspetti ' (He who has done the wrong awaits it).]

proverbs so misinterpreted ; had they refused to mitigate for us, so far as they could, the consequence of our errors. But if the words are taken in their true sense, as homely announcements of that law of divine retaliations in the world, according to which men shall eat of the fruit of their own doings, and be filled with their own ways, who shall gainsay them ? What affirm they more than every page of Scripture, every turn of human life, is affirming too, namely, that the everlasting order of God's universe cannot be violated with impunity, that there is a continual returning upon men of what they have done, and that in their history we may read their judgment ?

Charity begins at home, is the most obvious and familiar of these proverbs, selfishly abused. It may be, no doubt it often is, made the plea for a selfish withholding of assistance from all but a few, whom men may include in their ' at home, ' while sometimes the proverb receives a narrower inter-pretation still ; and self, and self only, is accounted to be ' at home '. And yet, in truth, what were that charity worth, which did *not* begin at home, which did *not* preserve the divine order and pro-portion and degree ? It is not for nothing that we have been grouped in families, neighbourhoods, and nations ; and he who will not recognize the divinely appointed nearnesses to himself of some over others, who thinks to be a cosmopolite with-out being a patriot, a philanthropist without own-ing a distinguishing love for them that are peculiarly ' his own ', who would thus have a circumference without a centre, deceives his own heart ; and affirming all men to be equally dear to him, is

T.E.P.   H

indeed affirming them to be equally indifferent. Home, the family, this is as the hearth at which the affections which are afterwards to go forth and warm in a larger circle, are themselves to be kept lively and warm ; and the charity which did not exercise itself in outcomings of kindness and love in the narrower, would be little likely to seek a wider range for itself. Wherever else it may *end*, and the larger the sphere which it makes for itself the better, it must yet *begin* at home *.

There are, again, proverbs which, from another point of view, might seem of an ignoble cast, and as calculated to lower the tone of morality among those who received them ; proposing as they do secondary, and therefore unworthy, motives to actions, which ought to be performed out of the highest. I mean such as this : *Honesty is the best policy ;* wherein honesty is commended, not because it is right, but because it is most prudent and politic, and has the promise of this present world. Now doubtless there are proverbs not a few which, like this, move in the region of what has been by Coleridge so well called ' prudential morality ', and did we accept them as containing the whole circle of motives to honesty or other right conduct, nothing could be worse, or more fitted to lower the moral standard of our lives. He who resolves to be honest because, and only because, it is *the best*

---

* In respect of other proverbs, such as the following, Tunica pallio propior ;—Frons occipitio prior [The coat is closer than the cloak ;—The forehead comes before the nape] ; I have greater doubt. The misuse lies nearer ; the selfishness may very probably be in the proverb itself, and not in our application of it ; though even these seem not incapable of a fair interpretation.

policy, will be little likely long to continue honest
at all. But the proverb does not pretend to usurp
the place of an ethical rule ; it does not presume to
cast down the higher law which should determine
to honesty and uprightness, that it may put itself
in its place ; it only declares that honesty, let alone
that it is the right thing, is also, even for this present world, the wisest. Nor dare we, let me further
add, despise prudential morality, such as is embodied in sayings like this. The motives which it
suggests are helps to a weak and tempted virtue,
may prove great assistances to it in some passing
moment of a violent temptation, however little
they can be regarded as able to make men *for a
continuance* even outwardly upright and just.

And once more, proverbs are not to be accounted
selfish, which announce selfishness ; unless they do
it, either avowedly recommending it as a rule and
maxim of life, or, if not so, yet with an evident
complacency and satisfaction in the announcement
which they make, and in this more covert and
perhaps still more mischievous way, taking part
with the evil which they proclaim. There are a
great many proverbs, which a lover of his race
would be very thankful if there had been nothing
in the world to justify or to provoke ; for the convictions they embody, the experiences on which
they rest must be regarded as very far from com-
plimentary to human nature : but seeing they
express that which is, however we might desire it
were not, it would be idle to wish them away, to
wish that this evil had not found its utterance.
Nay, it is much better that it should so have done ;
for thus taking form and shape, and being brought

directly under notice, it may be better watched against and avoided. Such proverbs, not selfish, but rather detecting selfishness and laying it bare, are the following ; this Russian, on the only too slight degree in which we are touched with other men's troubles : *The burden is light on the shoulders of another ;* with which the French may be compared : *One has always enough strength to bear the misfortunes of one's friends *.* Such is this Italian : *Every one draws the water to his own mill † ;* or as it appears in its eastern shape, which brings up the desert-bivouack before one's eyes : *Every one rakes the embers to his own cake.* Such this Latin, on the comparative wastefulness wherewith that which is another's is too often used : *Men cut broad thongs from other men's leather ‡ ;* with many more of the same character, which it would be only too easy to bring together.

With all this, I would not of course in the least deny that immoral proverbs, and only too many of them, exist. For if they are, as we have recognized them to be, the genuine transcript of what is stirring in the hearts of men, then, since there is cowardice, untruth, selfishness, unholiness, profaneness there, how should these be wanting here ? The world is not so consummate an hypocrite as the entire absence of all immoral proverbs would imply. There will be merely selfish ones, as our own : *Every one for himself, and God for us all ;*

* On a toujours assez de force pour supporter le malheur de ses amis. I confess this sounds to me rather like an imitation of Rochefoucault than a genuine proverb.

† Ognun tira l' acqua al suo molino.

‡ Ex alieno tergore lata secantur lora. [See p. 164.]

or as this Dutch : *Self's the man* * ; or more shame-lessly cynical still, as the French : *Better a grape for me, than two figs for thee*† ; or again, such as proclaim a doubt and disbelief in the existence of any high moral integrity anywhere, as *Every man has his price ;* or assume that poor men can scarcely be honest, as *It is hard for an empty sack to stand straight ;* or take it for granted that every man would cheat every other if he could, as the French : *Count after your father* ‡ ; or, if they do not actually ' speak good of the covetous ', yet assume it possible that a blessing can wait on that which a wicked covetousness has heaped together, as the Spanish : *Blessed is the son, whose father went to the devil ;* or find cloaks and apologies for sin, as the German : *Once is never* § ; or such as would imply that the evil of a sin lay not in its sinfulness, but in the outward disgrace annexed to it, as the Italian : *A sin concealed is half forgiven* ‖. Or again there will be proverbs dastardly and base,

---

* Zelf is de Man.

† J'aime mieux un raisin pour moi que deux figues pour toi.

‡ Comptez après votre père. Compare the Spanish : Entre dos amigos un notario y dos testigos [Between two friends let there be a notary and two witnesses].

§ Einmal, keinmal. This proverb was turned to such bad uses, that a German divine thought it necessary to write a treatise against it. There exists indeed several old works in German with such titles as the following, *Un-godly Proverbs a*n*d their Refutation*. It is not for nothing that Jeremy Taylor in one place gives this warning : ' Be curious to avoid all proverbs and propositions, or odd sayings, by which evil life is encouraged, and the hands of the spirit weakened.' In like manner Chrysostom (*Hom.* 73 in Matt.) denounces the Greek proverb : γλυκὺ ἤτω καὶ πνιξάτω [Let it be sweet though it choke me].

‖ Peccato celato, mezzo perdonato.

as the Spanish maxim of caution, which advises to *Draw the snake from its hole by another man's hand ;* to put, that is, another, and it may be for your own profit, to the peril from which you shrink yourself ;—or more dastardly still, ' scoundrel maxims ', an old English poet has called them ; as for instance, that one which is acted on only too often : *One must howl with the wolves* * ; in other words, when a general cry is raised against any, it is safest to join it, lest one be supposed to sympa- thise with its object ; to howl *with* the wolves, if one would not be hunted *by* them. In the whole circle of proverbs I know no baser, nor more das- tardly than this. And yet who will say that he has never traced in himself the cowardly temptation to obey it ? Besides these there will be, of which I shall spare you any examples, proverbs wanton and impure, and not merely proverbs thus earthly and sensual, but devilish ; such as some of those Italian on revenge which I quoted in my third lecture.

But for all this these immoral proverbs, rank weeds among the wholesome corn, are compara- tively rare. In the minority with all people, they are immeasurably in the minority with most. The fact is not a little worthy of our note. Surely there lies in it a solemn testimony, that however men may and do in their conduct continually violate the rule of right, yet these violations are ever felt to be such, are inwardly confessed not to be the law of man's life, but the transgressions of

---

* Badly turned into a rhyming pentameter :
    Consonus esto lupis, cum quibus esse cupis.
[Agree with the wolves if you want to live with them.]

the law ; and thus, stricken as with a secret shame,
and paying an unconscious homage to the majesty
of goodness, they do not presume to raise themselves into maxims, nor, for all the frequency with
which they may be repeated, pretend to claim
recognition as abiding standards of action.

As the sphere in which the proverb moves is no
imaginary world, but that actual and often very
homely world which is round us and about us ;
as it does not float in the clouds, but sets its feet
firmly on this common earth of ours from which
itself once grew, being occupied with present needs
and every-day cares, it is only natural that the
proverbs having reference to money should be
numerous ; and in the main it would be well if the
practice of the world rose to the height of its convictions as expressed in these. Frugality is connected with so many virtues—at least, its contrary
makes so many impossible—that the numerous
proverbial maxims inculcating this, than which
none perhaps are more frequent on the lips of men,
must be regarded as belonging to the better order *;
especially when taken with the check of others,
which forbid this frugality from degenerating
into a sordid and dishonourable parsimony ; such,
I mean, as our own : *The groat is ill-saved which
shames its master.* In how many the conviction
speaks out that the hastily-gotten will hardly be
the honestly-gotten, that ' he who makes haste to
be rich shall not be innocent ', as when the Spaniards

* ͵There are very few inculcating an opposite lesson :
this however is one : *Spend, and God will send ;* which
Howell glosses well : ' Yes, a bag and a wallet.'

say : *He who will be rich in a year, at the half-year they hang him* * ; in how many others, the confidence that the ill-won will also be the ill-spent †, that he who shuts up unlawful gain in his store-houses, is shutting up a fire that will one day destroy them. Very solemn and weighty in this sense is the German proverb : *The unrighteous penny corrupts the righteous pound* ‡ ; and the Spanish, too, is striking : *That which is another's always yearns for its lord* § ; it yearns, that is, to be gone and get to its true owner. In how many the conviction is expressed that this mammon, which more than anything else men are tempted to think God does not concern Himself about, is yet given and taken away by Him according to the laws of His righteousness ; given sometimes to His enemies and for their greater punishment, that under its fatal influence they may grow worse and worse, for *The more the carle riches, he wretches ;* but oftener withdrawn, because no due acknowledgment of Him was made in its use ; as when the German proverb declares : *Charity gives itself rich ; covetousness hoards itself poor* || ; and the Danish : *Give alms, that thy children may not ask them ;* and the Rabbis, with a yet deeper significance : *Alms are the salt of riches ;* the true anti-

---

* Quien en un año quiere ser rico, al medio le ahorcan.

† Male parta male dilabuntur [Naevius, *Danäe*.]—Wie gewonnen, so zerronnen. [Ill got ill gone.—Lightly come lightly go.]

‡ Ungerechter Pfennig verzehrt gerechten Thaler.

§ Lo ageno siempre pia por su dueño.

|| Der Geiz sammlet sich arm, die Milde giebt sich reich. In the sense of the latter half of this proverb *we* say, *Drawn wells are seldom dry ;* though this word is capable of very far wider application.

septic, which as such shall prevent them from themselves corrupting, and from corrupting those that have them ; which shall hinder them from developing a germ of corruption, such as shall in the end involve in one destruction them and their owners *.

At the same time, as it is the very character of proverbs to look at matters all round, there are others to remind us that even this very giving itself shall be with forethought and discretion ; with selection of right objects, and in right proportion to each. Teaching this, the Greeks said, *Sow with the hand, and not with the whole sack* † ; for as it fares with the seed corn, which if it shall prosper, must be providently dispersed with the hand, not prodigally shaken from the sack's mouth, so is it with benefits, which shall do good either to those who impart, or to those who receive them. Thus again, there is a Danish which says, *So give to-day, that thou shalt be able to give to-morrow ;*

---

* There is one remarkable Latin proverb on the moral cowardliness which it is the character of riches to generate, saying more briefly the same which Wordsworth said when he proclaimed

'that riches are akin

To fear, to change, to cowardice, and death' ;

it is this : Timidus Plutus : and has sometimes suggested to me the question whether he might not have had it in his mind when he composed his great sonnet in prospect of the invasion :

'These times touch monied worldlings with dismay' ;

not that his genius needed any such solicitation from without ; for the poem is only the natural outgrowth of that spirit and temper in which the whole series of noble and ennobling poems, the *Sonnets to Liberty*, is composed, and in perfect harmony with the rest ; yet is it, notwithstanding, in a very wonderful way shut up in the two words of the ancient proverb.

† Τῇ χειρὶ δεῖ σπείρειν, ἀλλὰ μὴ ὅλῳ τῷ θυλάκῳ.

and another : *So give to one, that thou shalt have to give to another* *.   And as closing this series, as teaching us in a homely but striking manner, with an image Dantesque in its vigour, that a man shall carry nothing away with him when he dieth, take this Italian, *Our last robe,* that is our winding sheet, *is made without pockets* †.

Let me further invite you to observe and to admire the prevailing tone of manliness which pervades the great body of the proverbs of all nations : let me urge you to take note how very few there are which would fain persuade you that ' luck is all ', or that your fortunes are in any other hands, under God, than your own. This our own proverb, *Win purple and wear purple,* proclaims.   There are some, but they are exceptions, to which the gambler, the idler, the so-called ' waiter upon Providence ', can appeal.   For the most part, however, they courageously accept the law of labour, *No pains, no gains,—No sweat, no sweet,—No mill, no meal* ‡, as the appointed law and condition of man's life.   *Where wilt thou go, ox, that thou wilt not have to plough?* § is the Catalan remonstrance addressed to one, who imagines by any outward change of circumstances to evade the inevitable task and toil of existence. And this is Turkish : *It is not with saying Honey,*

* Giv saa i Dag, at du og kandst give i morgen.—Giv een at du kand give en anden.

† L'ultimo vestito ce lo fanno senza tasche.

‡ This is the English form of that worthy old classical proverb : Φεύγων μύλον, ἄλφιτα φεύγει, or in Latin : Qui vitat molam, vitat farinam [Who shuns the mill shuns the flour].

§ Ahont anirás, bou, que no llaures ?   I prefer this form of it to the Spanish : Adonde yrá el buey, que no are ?

Honey, that sweetness will come into the mouth * ; and to many languages another with its striking image, *Sloth, the key of poverty* †, belongs : while, on the other hand, there are in almost all tongues such proverbs as the following : *God helps them that help themselves* ‡ : or as it appears with a slight variation in the Basque : *God is a good worker, but He loves to be helped.* And these proverbs, let me observe by the way, were not strange, in their import at least, to the founder of that religion which is usually supposed to inculcate a blind and indolent fatalism—however some who call themselves by his name may have forgotten the lesson which they convey. Certainly they were not strange to Mahomet himself ; if the following excellently-spoken word has been rightly ascribed to him. One evening, we are told, after a weary march through the desert, he was camping with his followers, and overheard one of them saying, ' I will loose my camel, and commit it to God ', on which Mahomet took him up : ' Friend, *tie* thy camel, and commit it to God § ; ' do, that is, whatever is thine to do, and then leave the issue in higher hands ; but till thou hast done this, till thou hast thus helped thyself, thou hast no right to look to Heaven to help thee.

[* Compare :—
       ' O who can hold a fire in his hand
       By thinking on the frosty Caucasus ?
       Or cloy the hungry edge of appetite
       By bare imagination of a feast ? '
          Shakespeare, *Richard II*, i. 3, 294–297.]
† Pereza, llave de pobreza.
‡ Dii facientes adjuvant.
§ According to the Spanish proverb : Quien bien ata, bien desata [='Safe bind, safe find'].

How excellently this unites genuine modesty and manly self-assertion : *Sit in your own place, and no man can make you rise ;* and how good is this Spanish, on the real dignity which there often is in doing things for ourselves, rather than in standing by and suffering others to do them for us : *Who has a mouth, let him not say to another, Blow* *. And as a part of this which I have called the manliness of proverbs, let me especially note the noble utterances which so many contain, summoning to a brave encountering of adverse fortune, to perseverance under disappointment and defeat and a long-continued inclemency of fate ; breathing as they do, a noble confidence that for the brave and bold the world will not always be adverse. *Where one door shuts another opens* † ; this belongs to too many nations to allow of our ascribing it especially to any one. And this Latin : *The sun of all days has not yet gone down* ‡ ; however, in its primary application intended for those who are at the top of Fortune's wheel, to warn them that they be not high-minded, for there is yet time for many a revolution in that wheel, is equally good for those at the bottom, and as it contains warning for those, so strength and encouragement for these ; for, as the Italians say : *The world is his who has patience* §. And then, to pass over some of our own, so familiar that they need not be adduced,

* Quien tiene boca, no diga á otro, Sopla.
† Donde una puerta se cierra, otra se abre.
‡ Nondum omnium dierum sol occidit.
§ Il mondo è, di chi ha pazienza.
    [' Wel abit that wel may tholye '
    (He well abides who can well endure).
            Proverbs of Hendyng (ab. 1280).]

how manful a lesson is contained in this Persian proverb : *A stone that is fit for the wall, is not left in the way.* It is a saying made for them who appear for a while to be overlooked, neglected, passed by ; who perceive in themselves capacities, which as yet no one else has recognized or cared to turn to account. Only *be fit for the wall ;* square, polish, prepare thyself for it ; do not limit thyself to the bare acquisition of such knowledge as is absolutely necessary for thy present position ; but rather learn languages, acquire useful information, stretch thyself out on this side and on that, cherishing and making much of whatever aptitudes thou findest in thyself ; and it is certain thy turn will come. Thou wilt not be *left in the way ;* sooner or later the builders will be glad of thee ; the wall will need thee to fill up a place in it, quite as much as thou needest a place to occupy in the wall. For the amount of real capacity in this world is so small, that places want persons to fill them quite as really as persons want to fill places ; although it must be allowed, they are not always as much aware of their want.

And this proverb, Italian and Spanish, *If I have lost the ring, yet the fingers are still here* *, is another of these brave utterances of which I have been speaking. In it is asserted the comparative indifference of that loss which reaches but to things external to us, so long as we ourselves remain, and are true to ourselves. *The fingers are* far more than *the ring :* if indeed those had gone, then *the man* would have been maimed ; but

* Se ben ho perso l'anello, ho pur anche le dita ;—Si se perdieron los anillos, aqui quedaron los dedillos.

another ring may come for that which has disappeared, or even with none the fingers will be fingers
still.   And as at once a contrast and complement
to this, take another, current among the free blacks
of Hayti, and expressing well the little profit which
there will be to a man in pieces of mere good luck,
which are no true outgrowths of anything which is
in him ; the manner in which, having no root in
himself out of which they grew, they will, as they
came to him by hazard, go from him by the same :
*The knife which thou hast found in the highway,
thou wilt lose in the highway* *.

But these numerous proverbs, urging self-
reliance, bidding us first to aid ourselves, if we
would have Heaven to aid us, must not be dismissed without a word or two at parting.   Prizing
them, as we well may, and the lessons which they
contain, at the highest, yet it will be profitable
for us at the same time always to remember that
to such there lies very near such a mischievous
perversion as this : ‘ Aid thyself, and thou wilt
need no other aid ’ ;   even as they have been
sometimes, no doubt, understood in this sense.
As, then, the pendant and counter-weight to them
all, not as unsaying what they have said, but as
fulfilling the other hemisphere in the complete orb
of truth, let me remind you of such also as the
following, often quoted or alluded to by Greek

---

* In their bastard French it runs thus : Gambette ous
trouvé nen gan chimin, nen gan chimin ous va pèdè li.
It may have been originally French, at any rate the French
have a proverb very much to the same effect : Ce qui vient
par la flute, s’en va par le tambour ; and compare the
modern Greek proverb : Ἀνεμομαζώματα, δαιμονσκορπίσματα
(What the wind gathers, the devil scatters).

and Latin authors : *The net of the sleeping (fisher-man) takes* * ;—a proverb the more interesting, that we have in the words of the Psalmist, (Ps. cxxvii. 2,) when accurately translated, a beautiful and perfect parallel : ' He giveth his beloved ' (not ' sleep ', as in our version, but) ' *in* sleep ' ; God's gifts gliding into his bosom, he knowing not how, and as little expecting as having laboured for them.   Of how many of the best gifts of every man's life will he not thankfully acknowledge this to have been true ; or, if he refuse to allow it, and will acknowledge no *eudæmonia*, no ' favour-able providence ' in his prosperities, but will see them all as of work, how little he deserves, how little likely he is, to retain them to the end.   Let us hold fast, then, this proverb as the most need-ful complement of those.

I feel that I should be wanting to hearers such as those who are assembled here, that I should fail in that purpose which has been, more or less, pre-sent to me even in dealing with the lighter portions of my subject, if I did not earnestly remind you of the many of these sayings that there are, which, while they have their lesson for all, yet seem more directly addressed to those standing, as not a few of us here, at the threshold of the more serious and earnest portion of their lives.   Lecturing to a

---

* Εὔδοντι κύρτος αἱρεῖ.—Dormienti rete trahit.   The reader with a *Plutarch's Lives* within his reach may turn to the very instructive little history told in connexion with this proverb, of Timotheus the Athenian commander ; an history which only requires to be translated into Christian language to contain a deep moral for all. (*Sulla,* c. 6.)

Young Men's Society, I shall not unfitly press these upon your notice. Take this Italian one, for instance : *When you grind your corn, give not the flour to the devil, and the bran to God ;*—in the distribution, that is, of your lives, apportion not your best years, your strength and your vigour to the service of sin and of the world, and only the refuse and rejected to your Maker, the wine to others, and the lees only to Him. Not so ; for there is another ancient proverb *, which we have made very well our own, and which in English runs thus : *It is too late to spare, when all is spent.* The words have obviously a primary application to the goods of this present life ; it is ill saving here, when nothing or next to nothing is left to save. But they are applied well by a heathen moralist, (and the application lies very near,) to those who begin to husband precious time, and to live for life's true ends, when life is nearly gone, is now at its dregs ; for, as he well urges, it is not the least only which remains at the bottom, but the worst †. On the other hand, *The morning hour has gold in its mouth* ‡ ; and this, true in respect of each of our days, in which the earlier hours given to toil will yield larger and more genial returns than the later, is true in a yet higher sense, of that great life-day, whereof all the lesser days of our life make up the moments, is true in respect of moral no less than mental acquisition. The *evening* hours have often only *silver* in their mouths

---

    * Sera in imo parsimonia.

    † Seneca (*Ep.* i.) : Non enim tantum *minimum* in imo, sed *pessimum* remanet.

    ‡ Morgenstund' hat Gold im Mund.

at the best. Nor is this Arabic proverb, as it appears to me, other than a very solemn one, being far deeper than at first sight it might seem : *Every day in thy life is a leaf in thy history* * ; a leaf which shall once be turned back to again, that it may be seen what was written there ; and that whatever *was* written may be read out in the hearing of all.

And among the proverbs having to do with a prudent ordering of our lives from the very first, this Spanish seems well worthy to be adduced : *That which the fool does in the end, the wise man does at the beginning* † ; the wise with a good grace what the fool with an ill ; the one to much profit what the other to little or to none. A word worth laying to heart ; for, indeed, that purchase of the Sibylline books by the Roman king, what a significant symbol it is of that which at one time or another, or, it may be, at many times, is finding place in almost every man's life ;—the same thing to be done in the end, the same price to be paid at the last, with only the difference, that much of the advantage, as well as all the grace, of an earlier compliance has passed away. The nine precious volumes have shrunk to six, and these dwindled to three, while yet the like price is demanded for the few as for the many ; for the remnant now as would once have made all our own.

I have already in a former lecture adduced a proverb which warns against a bad book as the worst of all robbers. In respect too of books

[* Emerson still more finely says : ' Every day is a day of judgment.']

† Lo que hace el loco á la postre, hace sabio al principio.

which are not bad, nay, of which the main staple
is good, but in which there is yet an admixture of
evil, as is the case with so many that have come
down to us from that old world not as yet partaker
of Christ, there is a proverb, which may very profitably accompany us in our study of all these :
Where the bee sucks honey, the spider sucks poison.
Very profitably may this word be kept in mind by
such as at any time are making themselves familiar
with the classical literature of antiquity, the great
writers of heathen Greece and Rome. How much
of noble, how much of elevating do they contain :
what love of country, what zeal for wisdom, may
be quickened in us by the study of them ; yea,
even to us Christians what intellectual, what large
moral gains will they yield.   Let the student be
as the bee looking for honey, and from the fields
and gardens of classical literature he may store it
abundantly in his hive.   And yet from this same
body of literature what poison is it possible to
draw ; what loss, through familiarity with evil, of
all vigorous abhorrence of it, till even the foulest
enormities shall come to be regarded with a specu-
lative curiosity rather than with an earnest hatred,
—yea, what lasting defilements of the imagination
and the heart may be contracted hence, till nothing shall be pure, the very mind and conscience
being defiled.   Let there come one whose sym-
pathies and affinities are with the poison and not
with the honey, and in these fields it will not be
impossible for him to find deadly flowers and weeds
from which he may suck poison enough.

With a few remarks on two proverbs more I
will bring this lecture to an end.   Here is one with

an insight at once subtle and profound into the heart of man : *Ill doers are ill deemers* * ; and instead of any commentary on this of my own, let me quote some words which were not intended to be a commentary upon it at all, and which furnish notwithstanding a better than any which I could hope to give. They are words of a great English divine of the seventeenth century, who is accounting for the offence which the Pharisee took at the Lord's acceptance of the affectionate homage and costly offering of the woman that was a sinner : ' Which familiar and affectionate officiousness, and sumptuous cost, together with that sinister fame that woman was noted with, could not but give much scandal to the Pharisees there present. For that dispensation of the law under which they lived making nothing perfect, but only curbing the outward actions of men ; it might very well be that they, being conscious to themselves of no better motions within than of either bitterness or lust, how fair soever they carried without, could not deem Christ's acceptance of so familiar and affectionate a service from a woman of that fame to proceed from anything better than some loose and vain principle . . . for by how much every one is himself obnoxious to temptation, by so much more suspicious he is that others transgress, when there

---

[* Compare Lord Tennyson's favourite saying, ' Men impute themselves'— *Life of,* vol. i. p. 269—and ' Shame take him that shame thinketh,' with the motto of the Order of the Garter, and the Italian, Chi mal pensa mal abbia. In Latin, ' Tuo ex ingenio mores alienos probas' —Plautus, *Truc.* ii. 47—' You judge others' characters by your own.']

is anything that may tempt out the corruptions of
a man * '

And in this Chinese proverb which follows,
*Better a diamond with a flaw, than a pebble without
one*, there is, to my mind, the assertion of a great
Christian truth, and of one which reaches deep
down to the very foundations of Christian morality, the more valuable as coming to us from a
people beyond the range and reach of the influ-
ences of direct Revelation. We may not be all
aware of the many and malignant assaults which
were made on the Christian faith, and on the
morality of the Bible, through the character of
David, by the blind and self-righteous Deists of a
century or more ago. Taking the Scripture testimony about him, that he was the man after God's
heart, and putting beside this the record of those
great sins which he committed, they sought to set
these great, yet still isolated, offences in the most
hateful light ; and thus to bring at once him, and
the Book which praised him, to a common shame.
But all this while, the question of *the man*, what
he was, and what the moral sum total of his life,
to which alone the Scripture testimony bore witness, and to which alone it was pledged, this was a
question with which they concerned themselves
not at all ; while yet it was a far more important
question than what any of his single acts may have

* Henry More, *On Godliness*, b. 8. How remarkable a
confirmation of the fact asserted in that proverb and in
this passage lies in the twofold uses of the Greek word
κακοήθεια ; having, for its first meaning, an evil disposition
in a man's self, it has for its second an interpreting on his
part for the worst of all the actions of other men.
[Compare the monkish line, "Autumat hoc in me quod
novit perfidus in se."]

been ; and it was this which, in the estimate of his character, was really at issue. To this question *we* answer, *a diamond,* which, if a diamond *with a flaw,* as are all but the one ' entire and perfect chrysolite ', would yet outvalue a mountain of *pebbles without one,* such as they were ; even assuming the pebbles to *be* without ; and not merely to *seem* so, because their flaw was an all-pervading one, and only not so quickly detected, inasmuch as the contrast was wanting of any clearer material which should at once reveal its presence.

THE THEOLOGY OF PROVERBS

I sought, as best I could, in my last lecture to furnish you with some helps for estimating the ethical worth of proverbs. Their theology alone remains ; the aspects, that is, under which they contemplate, not now any more man's relations with his fellow-man, but those on which in the end all others must depend, his relations with God. Between the subject matter, indeed, of that lecture and of this I have found it nearly impossible to draw any very accurate line of distinction. Much which was there might nearly as fitly have been here ; some which I have reserved for this might already have found its place there. It is this, however, which I propose more directly to consider, namely, what proverbs have to say concerning the moral government of the world, and, more important still, concerning its Governor ? How does all this present itself to the popular mind and conscience, as attested by these ? What, in short, is their theology ? for such, good or bad, it is evident that abundantly they have.

Here, as everywhere else, their testimony is a mingled one. The darkness, the error, the confusion of man's heart, out of which he oftentimes sees distortedly, and sometimes sees not at all, have all embodied themselves in his word. Yet still, as it is the very nature of the false, in its separate manifestations, to resolve into nothingness, though only to be succeeded by new births in a like kind, while the true abides and continues, it has thus come to pass that we have generally in those utterances on which the stamp of permanence has been set, the nobler voices, the truer faith of humanity, in respect of its own destinies and of Him by whom those destinies are ordered.

I would not hesitate to say that the great glory of proverbs in this their highest aspect, and that which makes many of them so full of blessing to those who cordially accept them, is the conviction of which they are full, that, despite all appearances to the contrary, this world is God's world, and not the world of the devil, or of those wicked men who may be prospering for an hour; there is nothing in them so precious as their faith that in the long run it will approve itself to be such : which being so, that it must be well in the end with the doer of the right, the speaker of the truth ; no blind ' whirligig of time ', but the hand of the living God, in due time ' bringing round its revenges '. It is impossible to estimate too highly their bold and clear proclamation of this conviction ; for it is, after all, the belief of this or the denial of this, on which everything in the life of each one of us turns. On this depends whether we shall separate ourselves from the world's falsehood and evil, and do vigorous battle against them ; or acquiesce in, and be ourselves absorbed by, them.

Listen to proverbs such as these ; surely they are penetrated with the assurance that one who,

Himself being The Truth, will make truth in small and in great to triumph at the last, is ruling over all : and first, hear a proverb of our own : *A lie has no legs ;* it is one true alike in its humblest application and its highest ; be the lie the miserable petty falsehood which disturbs a family or a neighbourhood for a day ; or one of the larger frauds, the falsehoods not in word only but in act, to which a longer date and a far larger sphere are assigned, which for a time seem to fill the world, and to carry everything in triumph before them. Still the lie, in that it is a lie, always carries within itself the germs of its own dissolution. It is sure to destroy itself at last. Its priests may prop it up from without, may set it on its feet again, after it has once fallen before the presence of the truth, yet this all will be labour in vain ; it will only be, like Dagon, again to fall, and more shamefully and more irretrievably than before *. On the other hand, the vivacity of the truth, as contrasted with this short-lived character of the lie, is well expressed in a Swiss proverb : *It takes a good many shovelfuls of earth to bury the truth.* For, bury it

* Perhaps the Spanish form of this proverb is still better : La mentira tiene *cortas* las piernas [A lie has *short* legs] ; for the lie does go, though not far. Compare the French : La vérité, comme l'huile, vient au dessus [Truth, like oil, comes to the top. Compare the German, ' Zum Begräbniss der wahrheit gehören viel Schaufeln ' (It takes a good many shovelfuls to bury the truth).
    ' Truth crushed to earth shall rise again :
    The eternal years of God are hers.'—
               Bryant, *The Battle-field.*
    ' Thou (Truth) diest not,
No one has seen thy monument, nor shall.'
               H. Bonar.
See I Esdras, iv. 38–41.]

as deep as men may, it will have a resurrection notwithstanding. They may roll a great stone, and seal the sepulchre in which it is laid, and set a watch upon it, yet still, like its Lord, it comes forth again at its appointed hour. It cannot die, being of an immortal race ; for, as the Spanish proverb nobly declares, *The truth is daughter of God* *.

Again, consider this proverb : *Tell the truth, and shame the devil.* It is one which will well repay a few thoughtful moments bestowed on it, and the more so, because, even while we instinctively feel its truth, the deep moral basis on which it rests may yet not reveal itself to us at once. Nay, the saying may seem to contradict the actual experience of things ; for how often telling the truth —confessing, that is, some great fault, taking home to ourselves, it may be, some grievous sin—would appear anything rather than shaming the devil ; shaming indeed ourselves, but rather bringing glory to him, whose glory, such as it is, is in the sin and shame of men. And yet the word is true, and deeply true, notwithstanding. The element of lies is that in which alone he who is ' the father of them ' lives and thrives. So long then as a wrong-doer presents to himself, or seeks to present to others, the actual facts of his conduct different from what they really are, conceals, palliates, denies them,—so long, in regard of that man, Satan's kingdom stands. But so soon as the things concerning himself are seen and owned by a man as they indeed exist in God's sight, as they are when weighed in the balances of the eternal righteousness ; when once a man has brought himself to

* La verdad es hija de Dios.

tell the truth to himself, and, where need requires, to others also, then having done, and in so far as he has done this, he has abandoned the devil's standard, he belongs to the kingdom of the truth ; and as belonging to it he may rebuke, and does rebuke and put to shame all makers and lovers of a lie, even to the very prince of them all. ' Give glory to God ' was what Joshua said to Achan, when he would lead him to confess his guilt. This is but the other and fairer side of the tapestry ; this is but *shame the devil,* on its more blessed side.

Once more ;—the Latin proverb, *The voice of the people, the voice of God* *, is one which it is well worth our while to understand. If it were affirmed in this that every outcry of the multitude, sup- posing only it be loud enough and wide enough, ought to be accepted as the voice of God speaking through them, no proposition more foolish or more impious could well be imagined. But *the voice of the people* is something very different from this. The proverb rests on the assumption that the foundations of man's being are laid in the truth ; from which it will follow, that no conviction which is really a conviction of the universal humanity, but reposes on a true ground ; no faith, which is indeed the faith of mankind, but has a reality cor- responding to it : for, as Jeremy Taylor has said : ' It is not a vain noise, when many nations join their voices in the attestation or detestation of an action ' ; and Hooker : ' The general and per- petual voice of men is as the sentence of God Him- self. For that which all men have at all times learned, nature herself must needs have taught ;

* Vox populi, vox Dei.

and God being the author of nature, her voice is but His instrument '. (*Eccles. Pol., b.* i. § 8.) * The task and difficulty, of course, must ever be to discover what this faith and what these convictions are ; and this can only be done by an induction from a sufficient number of facts, and in sufficiently different times, to enable us to feel confident that we have indeed seized that which is the constant quantity of truth in them all, and separated this from the inconstant one of falsehood and error, evermore offering itself in its room ; that we have not taken some momentary cry, wrung out by interest, by passion, or by pain, for *the voice of God ;* but claimed this august title only for that true voice of humanity, which, unless everything be false, we have a right to assume an echo of the voice of God.

Thus, to take an example, the natural horror everywhere felt in regard of marriages contracted between those very near in blood, has been always and with right appealed to as a potent argument against such unions. The induction is so large, that is, the nations who have agreed in entertaining this horror are so many, oftentimes nations disagreeing in almost everything besides ; the times during which this instinctive revolt against such unions has been felt, extend through such long ages ; that the few exceptions, even where they are of civilized nations, as of the Egyptians who married their sisters, or of the Persians, among whom marriages more dreadful still were permitted,

[* Compare the *dictum* of Augustine which weighed so potently with Newman, ' Securus orbis judicat ' (The judgment of the world is sure to be right)—*Apologia,* p. 116.]

cannot be allowed any weight ; and, of course, still less the exception of any savage tribe, in which all that constitutes the human in humanity has now disappeared. These exceptions can only be regarded as violations of the divine order of man's life ; not as evidences that we have falsely imagined an order where there was none. Here is a true *voice of the people ;* and on the grounds laid down above, we have a right to assume this to be a *voice of God* as well. And so too, with respect to the existence of a First Cause, Creator and Upholder of all things, the universal consent and conviction of all people, the *consensus gentium,* must be considered of itself a mighty evidence in its favour ; a testimony which God is pleased to render to Himself through His creatures. This man or that, this generation or the other, might be deceived, but all men and all generations could not ; the *vox populi* makes itself felt as a *vox Dei.* The existence here and there of an atheist no more disturbs our conclusion that it is of the essence of man's nature to believe in a God, than do such monstrous births as from time to time find place, children with two heads or with no arms, shake our assurance that it is the normal condition of man to have one head and two arms.

This last is one of the proverbs which may be said to belong to the Apology for Natural Religion. There are others, of which it would not be farfetched to affirm that they belong to the Apology for Revealed. Thus it was very usual with Voltaire and other infidels of his time to appeal to the present barrenness and desolation of Palestine, in proof that it could never have supported the vast population which the Scripture everywhere assumes or affirms. A proverb in the language of the arch-scoffer himself might, if he had given heed to it, have put him on the right track, had he wished to be put upon it, for understanding how this could have been : *As the man is worth, his land is worth* *. Man is lord of his outward condition to a far greater extent than is commonly assumed ; even climate, which seems at first sight so completely out of his reach, it is his immensely to modify ; and if nature stamps herself on him, he stamps himself yet more powerfully on nature. It is not a mere figure of speech, that of the Psalmist, ' A fruitful land maketh He barren for the wickedness of them that dwell therein '. (Ps. cvii. 34.) God makes it barren, and ever less capable of nourishing its inhabitants ; but He makes it so through the sloth, the indolence, the shortsightedness of those that should have dressed and kept it. In the condition of a land may be found the echo, the reflection, the transcript of the moral and spiritual condition of those that should cultivate it : where one is waste, the other will be waste also. Under the desolating curse of Mohammedan domination the fairest portions of the earth have gone back from a garden to a wilderness : but only let that people for whom Palestine is yet destined return to it again, and return a righteous nation, and in a little while all the descriptions of its earlier fertility will be more than borne out by its later, and it will easily sustain its millions again.

How many proverbs, which cannot be affirmed

* Tant vaut l'homme, tant vaut sa terre.

to have been originally made for the kingdom of heaven, do yet in their highest fulfilment manifestly belong to it, so that it seems as of right to claim that for its own, even as it claims, or rather reclaims, whatever else is good or true in the world, the seeds of truth wherever dispersed abroad, as belonging rightfully to itself.   Thus there is that beautiful proverb, of which Pythagoras is reputed the author :   *The things of friends are in common* *.
Where does this find its exhaustive fulfilment, but in the communion of saints, their communion not with one another merely, though indeed this is a part of its fulfilment, but in their communion with Him, who is the friend of all good men ?   That such a conclusion lay legitimately in the words Socrates plainly saw ; who argued from it, that since good men were the friends of the gods, therefore whatever things were the gods', were also theirs ; being, when he thus concluded, as near as one who had not the highest light of all, could be to that great word of the Apostle's, ' All things are yours '.

Nor can I otherwise than esteem the ancient proverb as a very fine one, and one which we may gladly claim for our own : *Many meet the gods, but few salute them* †. How often do the gods (for I will keep in the language which this proverb suggests and supplies) *meet* men in the shape of a sorrow which might be a purifying one, of a joy

---

* Κοινὰ τὰ τῶν φίλων. [See A. E. Chaignet, *Pythagore*, i.102.]
[† Occurrit cuicunque Deus pauciquesalutant. Compare Ovid's charming episode of Baucis and Philemon (*Metamorphoses*) and Gerald Massey's lines—
' We may not see God's face, yet at our side
  He combats for us with his vizor down.']

which might elevate their hearts to thankfulness
and praise ; in a sickness or a recovery, a disappointment or a success ; and yet how few, as it
must be sadly owned, *salute* them ; how few recognise their august presences in this joy or this
sorrow, this blessing added, or this blessing taken
away. As this proverb has reference to men's
failing to *see* the Divine presences, so let me observe by the way, there is a very grand French one
which expresses the same truth, under the image
of a failing to *hear* the divine voices, those voices
being drowned by the deafening hubbub of the
world : *The noise is so great, one cannot hear
God thunder* *.

Here is another proverb which the Church has
long since claimed, at least in its import, for her
own : *One man, no man* †. I should find it very
hard indeed to persuade myself that whoever
uttered it first, attached to it no deeper meaning
than Erasmus gives him credit for—namely, that
nothing important can be effected by a single man,
destitute of the help of his fellows ‡. The word is
a far more profound one than this, and rests on
that great truth upon which the deeper thinkers
of antiquity laid so much stress—namely, that *in
the idea* the state precedes the individual, man
not being merely accidentally *gregarious*, but
essentially *social*. The solitary man, it would say,
is a monstrous conception, so utterly maimed and
crippled must he be ; the condition of solitariness

---

* Le bruit est si fort, qu'on n'entend pas Dieu tonner.
† Εἶs ἀνὴρ, οὐδεὶs ἀνήρ.
‡ Sensus est nihil egregium præstari posse ab uno
homine, omni auxilio destituto.

involving so entire a suppression of all which belongs to the development of that wherein the true
idea of humanity resides, of all which differences
man from the beasts of the field ; and in this sense
One man is *no man ;* and this, I am sure, the proverb from the first intended.   Nor may we stop
here.   This word is capable of, and seems to
demand a still higher application to man as a
destined member of the kingdom of heaven.   But
he can only be in training for this, when he is,
and regards himself, as not alone, but the member
of a family.   As *one man* he is *no man ;* and the
strength and value of what is called Church
teaching is greatly this, that it does recognise and
realize this fact, that it contemplates and deals
with the faithful man, not as isolated, but as one
of an organic body, with duties which flow as
moral necessities from his position therein ;   rather
than by himself, and as one whose duties to others
are indeed only the exercise of private graces for
his own benefit.   And all that are called Church
doctrines, when they really understand themselves, have their root and their real strength in
that great truth which this proverb declares, that
One man is no man, that only in a fellowship and
communion is or can any man be aught.

And then there is another proverb, which Plato
so loved to quote against the sophists, the men who
flattered and corrupted the nobler youth of Athens,
promising to impart to them easy short cuts to the
attainment of wisdom and knowledge and philosophy ;   and this, without demanding the exercise
of any labour or patience or self-denial on their
parts.   But with the proverb, *Good things are*

hard *, he continually rebuked their empty pretensions ; with this he made at least suspicious their promises ; and this proverb, true in the sense wherein Plato used it, and that sense was earnest and serious enough, yet surely reappears, glorified and transfigured, but recognisable still, in the Saviour's words : ' The kingdom of heaven is taken by violence, and the violent take it by force '†.

---

* Χαλεπὰ τὰ καλά.

† The deepening of a proverb's use among Christian nations as compared with earlier applications of the same may be illustrated by an example, which however, as not being directly theological, and thus not bearing immediately upon the matter in hand, I shall prefer to append in a note. An old Greek and Latin proverb, *A great city, a great solitude* (Magna civitas, magna solitudo) seems to have dwelt merely on the outside of things, and to have meant no more than this, namely, that a city ambitiously laid out and upon a large scheme would with difficulty find inhabitants sufficient, would wear an appearance of emptiness and desolation ; as there used to be a jest about Washington, that strangers would sometimes imagine themselves deep in the woods, when indeed they were in the centre of the city. But with deeper cravings of the human heart after love and affection, the proverb was claimed in an higher sense. We may take in proof these striking words of De Quincey, which are the more striking that neither they nor the context contain any direct reference to the proverb : ' No man,' he says, ' ever was left to himself for the first time in the streets, as yet unknown, of London, but he must have felt saddened and mortified, perhaps terrified, by the sense of desertion and utter loneliness which belongs to his situation. No loneliness can be like that which weighs upon the heart in the centre of faces never ending, without voice or utterance for him ; eyes innumerable that have " no speculation " in their orbs which *he* can understand ; and hurrying figures of men and women weaving to and fro, with no apparent purposes intelligible to a stranger, seeming like a masque of maniacs, or a pageant of shadowy illusions.' A direct reference to the proverb is to be found in some affecting words of Lord Bacon, who glosses and explains it exactly in this sense : ' For a crowd is not company, and faces

T.E.P.   K

This method of looking in proverbs for an higher meaning than any which lies on their surface, or which they seem to bear on their fronts ; or rather of searching out their highest intention, and claiming that as their truest, even though it should not be that perceived in them by most, or that which lay nearest to them at their first generation, is one that will lead us in many interesting paths. And it is not merely those of heathen antiquity which shall thus be persuaded often, and that without any forcing, to render up a Christian meaning ; but (as was indeed to be expected) still more often those of a later time, even those which the world had seemed to claim for its own, shall be found to move in a spiritual sphere as their truest. Let me offer in evidence of this these four or five, which come to us from Italy : *He who has love in his heart, has spurs in his sides ;—Love rules without law ;—Love rules his kingdom without a sword ;—Love knows nothing of Labour ;—Love is the master of all arts* *. Take these, even with the necessary drawbacks of my English translation ; but still more, in their original beauty ; and how exquisitely do they set forth, in whatever light you regard them, the free creative impulses of love, its delight to labour and to serve ; how worthily do they glorify the kingdom of love as

are but a gallery of pictures, and talk but a tinkling cymbal, where there is no love.'
    * Chi ha l'amor nel petto, ha lo sprone a i fianchi.—Amor regge senza legge. (Cf. Rom. xiii. 9, 10.)—Amor regge il suo regno senza spada.—Amor non conosce travaglio. (Cf. Gen. xxix. 20, 30.)—Di tutte le arti maestro è amore.—Di tutto condimento è amore. [Love gives a relish to everything ; these furnish the inspiring *motif* of V. Hugo's *Travailleurs de Mer.*]

the only kingdom of a free and joyful obedience. While yet at the same time, if we would appreciate them at *all* their worth, is it possible to stop short of an application of them to that kingdom of love, which, because it is in the highest sense such, is also a kingdom of heaven ? And then, what precious witness do these utterances contain, the more precious as current among a people nursed in the theology of Rome, against the shameless assertion that selfishness is the only motive sufficient to produce good (?) works : for in such an assertion the Romish impugners of a free justification constantly deal ; evermore charging this that we hold, of our justification by faith only, (which, when translated into the language of ethics, is at least as important in the province of morality as it is in that of theology,) with being an immoral doctrine, and not so fruitful in deeds of love as one which should connect these deeds with a selfish thought of promoting our own safety thereby.

There are proverbs which reach the height of evangelical morality. ' Little gospels ' * the Spaniard has somewhat too boldly entitled his ; and certainly there are many which at once we feel could nowhere have arisen or obtained circulation but under the influence of Christian faith, being in spirit, and often in form no less than in spirit, the outbirths of it. Thus is it with that exquisitely beautiful proverb of our own : *The way to heaven is by Weeping-Cross* † ; nor otherwise with the Span-

---

* Evangelios pequeños.

† Der Weg zum Himmel geht durch Kreuzdorn. Compare the medieval obverse of the same : Via Crucis, via lucis.

ish : *God never wounds with both hands* * ; not with *both*, for He ever reserves one with which to bind up and to heal. And another Spanish, evidently intended to give the sum and substance of all which in life is to be desired the most, *Peace and patience, and death with penitence* †, gives this sum certainly only as it presents itself to the Christian eye. And this of ours is Christian both in form and in spirit : *Every cross hath its inscription*—the name, that is, inscribed upon it, of the person for whom it was shaped ; it was intended for those shoulders upon which it is laid, and will adapt itself to them ; that fearful word is never true which a spirit greatly vexed spake in the hour of its impatience : ' I have little faith in the paternal love which I need ; so ruthless, or so negligent seems the government of this earth ' ‡.

So too is it with that ancient German proverb : *When God loathes aught, men presently loathe it too* §. He who first uttered this must have been one who had watched long the ways by which shame and honour travel in this world ; and in this watching must have noted how it ever came to pass that even worldly honour tarried not long with them from whom the true honour which cometh from God had departed. For the worldly

---

* No hiere Dios con dos manos.

† Paz y paciencia, y muerte con penitencia.

‡ *Memoirs of Margaret Fuller*, vol. iii. p. 266. In respect of words like these, wrung out from moments of agony, and not the abiding convictions of the utterer, may we not venture to hope that our own proverb, *For mad words deaf ears*, is often graciously true, even in the very courts of heaven ?

§ Wenn Gott ein Ding verdreusst, so verdreusst es auch bald die Menschen.

honour is but a shadow and reflex that waits upon the heavenly ; it may indeed linger for a little, but it will be only for a little, after it is divorced from its substance. Where the honour from Him has been withdrawn, He causes in one way or another the honour from men ere long to be withdrawn too. When He loathes, presently man loathes also. The saltless salt is not merely cast out by Him, but is trodden under foot of *men.* (Matt. v. 13.) A Louis the Fifteenth's death-bed is in its way as hideous to the natural as it is to the spiritual eye *.

We are told of the good Sir Matthew Hale, who was animated with a true zeal for holiness, an earnest desire to walk close to God, that he had continually in his mouth the modern Latin proverb, *We perish by permitted things* †. Assuredly it is one very well worthy to be of all remembered, searching as it does into the innermost secrets of men's lives. It is no doubt true that nearly as much danger threatens the soul from things permitted as from things unpermitted ; in some respects more danger ; for these being disallowed altogether, do not make the insidious approaches of those, which, coming in under allowance, do yet so easily slip into dangerous excess.

---

* The following have all a right to be termed Christian proverbs : Chi non vuol servir ad un solo Signor, à molti ha da servir ;—E padron del mondo chi lo disprezza, schiavo chi lo apprezza ;—[Span.] Quando Dios quiere, con todos vientos llueve [He who is not willing to serve one Lord will have to serve many ;—He is the world's master who despises it, its slave who prizes it ;—When God wills it rains with every wind].

† Perimus licitis.

It would be interesting to collect, as with reverence one might, variations on scriptural proverbs or sayings, which the proverbs of this world supply ; and this, both in those cases where the latter have grown out of the former, owing more nearly or more remotely their existence to them, and in those also where they are independent of them,—so far, that is, as anything true can be independent of the absolute Truth. Some of those which follow evidently belong to one of these classes, some to the other. Thus Solomon has said : ' It is better to dwell in the corner of the housetop than with a brawling woman in a wide house ' (Prov. xxi. 9) ; and again : ' Better a dry morsel and quietness therewith, than an house full of sacrifices with strife ' (Prov. xvii. 1). With these compare the two proverbs, a Latin and Spanish, adduced below *. The Psalmist has said : ' As he loved cursing, so let it come unto him ' (Ps. cix. 17). The Turks express their faith in this same law of the divine retaliations : *Curses, like chickens, always come home to roost :* they return, that is, to those from whom they went forth ; while in the Yoruba language there is a proverb to the same effect : *Ashes always fly back in the face of him that throws them ;* while our own, *Harm watch, harm catch,* and the Spanish, *Who sows thorns, let him not walk barefoot* †, are utterances of very

* Non quam late sed quam læte habites, refert.—Mas vale un pedazo de pan con amor, que gallinas con dolor [It matters not how large but how cheerful your home is.—A morsel of bread with love is better than a fowl with grief].

† Quien siembra abrojos, no ande descalzo. Compare the Latin : Si vultur es, cadaver expecta [If thou

nearly the same conviction. Our Lord declares, that without His Father there falls no single sparrow to the ground, that 'not one of them is forgotten before God.' (Luke xii. 6.) The same truth of a *providentia specialissima*, (between which and no providence at all there is indeed no tenable position,) is asserted in the Catalan proverb : *No leaf moves, but God wills it* *. Again, He has said : 'No man can serve two masters.' (Matt. vi. 24.) And the Spanish proverb : *He who must serve two masters, must lie to one* †. Or compare with Matt. xix. 29, this remarkable Arabic proverb : *Purchase the next world with this ; so shalt thou win both.* He has spoken of 'mammon of unrighteousness'—indicating hereby, in Leighton's words, ' that iniquity is so involved in the notion of riches, that it can very hardly be separated from them,'‡ and this phrase Jerome illustrates by a proverb that would not otherwise have reached us ; 'that saying,' he says, ' appears true to me : *A rich man is either himself an unjust one, or the heir of one* '§. Again, the Lord has said :

are a vulture look out for carrion]; and the French : Maudissons sont feuilles ; qui les sème, il les recueille [Curses are leaves ; he who scatters them must gather them].

* No se mou la fulla, que Deu no ha vulla. This is one of the proverbs of which the peculiar grace and charm nearly disappears in the rendering.

† Quien à dos señores ha de servir, al uno ha de mentir.

[‡ Compare : ' As a nail sticketh fast between the joinings of the stones, so doth sin stick close between buying and selling.'—Ecclus. xxvii. 2.]

§ Verum mihi videtur illud : Dives aut iniquus, aut iniqui hæres. Out of a sense of the same, as I take it, the striking Italian proverb had its rise : Mai diventò fiume grande, chi non v' entrasse acqua torbida [There is never a great river but some muddy water gets into it].

' Many be called, but few chosen ' (Matt. xx. 16) ; many have the outward marks of a Christian profession, few the inner substance. Some early Christian Fathers loved much to bring into comparison with this a Greek proverb, spoken indeed quite independently of it, and long previously ; and the parallel certainly is a singularly happy one : *The thyrsus-bearers are many, but the bacchants few* * ; many assume the signs and outward tokens of inspiration, whirling the thyrsus aloft ; but those whom the god indeed fills with his spirit are few all the while †. With our Lord's words concerning the mote and the beam (Matt. vii. 3, 5) compare this Chinese proverb : *Sweep away the snow from thine own door, and heed not the frost upon thy neighbour's tiles.*

It has been sometimes a matter of consideration to me whether we of the clergy might not make larger use, though of course it would be only occasional, of proverbs in our public teaching than

---

* Πολλοί τοι ναρθηκοφόροι, παῦροι δέ τε βάκχοι.

† The fact which this proverb proclaims, of a great gulf existing between what men profess and what they are, is one too frequently repeating itself and thrusting itself on the notice of all, not to have found its utterance in an infinite variety of forms, although none perhaps so deep and poetical as this. Thus there is another Greek line, fairly represented by this Latin :
Qui tauros stimulent multi, sed rarus arator
[Many a one can goad the oxen, but ploughmen are scarce];
and there is the classical Roman proverb : Non omnes qui habent citharam, sunt citharœdi [Not all are harpers who possess a harp]; and the medieval rhyming verse :
Non est venator quivis per cornua flator
[Not every one who blows a horn is a huntsman];
and this Eastern word : *Hast thou mounted the pulpit, thou art not therefore a preacher ;* with many more.

we do. Great popular preachers of time past, or, seeing that this phrase has now so questionable a sound, great preachers for the people, such as have found their way to the universal heart of their fellows, addressing themselves not to that which some men had different from others, but to that rather which each had in common with all, have been ever great employers of proverbs. Thus he who would know the riches of those in the German tongue, with the vigorous manifold employment of which they are capable, will find no richer mine to dig in than the works of Luther. And such employment of them would, I believe, with our country congregations, be especially valuable. Any one, who by after investigation has sought to discover how much our rustic hearers carry away, even from the sermons to which they have attentively listened, will find that it is hardly ever the course and tenor of the argument, supposing the discourse to have contained such ; but if anything was uttered, as it used so often to be by the best puritan preachers, tersely, pointedly, epigrammatically, this will have stayed by them, while all beside has passed away. Now, the merits of terseness and point, which have caused other words to be remembered, are exactly those which signalize the proverb, and generally in a yet higher degree.

It need scarcely be observed, that, if thus used, they will have to be employed with prudence and discretion, and with a careful selection. Thus, even with the example of so grave a divine as Bishop Sanderson before me, I should hesitate to employ in a sermon such a proverb as *Over shoes*, *over boots*—one which he declares to be the motto of some, who having advanced a certain way in sin, presently become utterly wretchless, caring not, and counting it wholly indifferent, how much further in evil they advance. Nor would I exactly recommend such use of a proverb as St. Bernard makes, who, in a sermon on the angels, desiring to shew *à priori* the extreme probability of their active and loving ministries in the service of men, adduces the Latin proverb : *Who loves me, loves my dog* * ; and proceeds to argue thus ; We are the dogs under Christ's table ; the angels love Him, they therefore love us.

But, although not exactly thus, the thing, I am persuaded, might be done, and with profit. Thus, in a discourse warning against sins of the tongue, there are many words which we might produce of our own to describe the mischief it inflicts that would be flatter, duller, less likely to be remembered than the old proverb : *The tongue is not steel, but it cuts.*† On God's faithfulness in sustaining, upholding, rewarding his servants, there are feebler things which we might bring out of our own treasure-house, than to remind our hearers of that word : *He who serves God, serves a good Master.*

---

* Qui me amat, amat et canem meum. (*In Fest. S. Mich. Serm.* I, § 3.)

[† Suggested probably by ' The stroke of the tongue breaketh the bones. Many have fallen by the edge of the sword, but not so many as have fallen by the tongue.' —*Ecclus.* xxviii. 17, 18. Compare ' Tonge breketh bon and nath (hath not) hire selue non.'—*Proverbs of Hendyng*, l. 144.

' Tongue breaketh bone and itselfe hath none.'
Parlament of Byrdes, ab. 1550.
See F. E. Hulme, *Proverb Lore*, p. 199.]

And this one might sink deep, telling of the enemy whom every one of us has the most to fear : *No man has a worse friend than he brings with him from home.* It stands in striking agreement with Augustine's remarkable prayer ' Deliver me from the evil man, from myself ' *. Or again : *Ill weeds grow apace* †;—with how lively an image does this set forth to us the rank luxuriant up-growth of sinful lusts and desires in the garden of an uncared-for, untended heart. I know not whether we might presume sufficient quickness of apprehension on the part of our hearers to venture on the folowing : *The horse which draws its halter is not quite escaped ;* but I can hardly imagine an happier illustration of the fact, that so long as any remnant of a sinful habit is retained by us, so long as we draw this halter, we make but an idle boast of our liberty ; we may, by means of that which we still drag with us, be at any moment again entangled altogether in the bondage from which we seemed to have entirely escaped.

In every language some of its noblest proverbs, such as oftentimes are admirably adapted for this application of which I am speaking, are those embodying men's confidence in God's moral government of the world, in His avenging righteousness, however much there may be in the confusions of

---

* Libera me ab homine malo, a meipso.
[† In French : ' Mauvaise herbe croit toujours ' ; in Italian : ' Erba mala preste cresce'. Old versions are : ' Ewyl weed ys sone y-growe ' (Harl. MS. ab. 1490) ; and

' Ill weede groweth fast whereby the corne is lorne,
For surely the weed overgroweth the corn.'
F. E Hulme, *Proverb Lore*, p. 12.]

the present evil time to provoke a doubt or even a denial of this. Thus, *Punishment is lame, but it comes,* which, if not old, yet rests on an image derived from antiquity, is good ; although inferior in every way, in energy of expression, as in fulness of sense, to the ancient Greek one : *The mill of God grinds late, but grinds to powder* * ; for this brings in the further thought, that His judgments, however long they tarry, yet, when they arrive, are crushing ones. There is indeed another of our own, not unworthy to be set beside this, announcing, though with quite another image, the same fact of the tardy but terrible arrivals of judgment : *God comes with leaden feet, but strikes with iron hands.* And then, how awfully sublime another which has come down to us as part of the wisdom of the ancient heathen world : I mean the following : *The feet of the (avenging) deities are shod with wool* †. Here a new thought is introduced,—the noiseless approach and advance of these judgments, as noiseless as the steps of one whose feet were wrapped in wool,—the manner in which they overtake secure sinners even in the hour of their utmost security. Who that has udied the history of the great crimes and criminals of the world, but will with a shuddering awe set his seal to the truth of

---

* Ὀψὲ Θεῶν ἀλέουσι μύλοι, ἀλέουσι δὲ λεπτά. [This proverb is found in Plutarch, and is quoted by Origen, *Against Celsus,* bk. viii. ch. 40. Compare Plutarch, ' *On the Delays in the Divine Justice.*'—Trench, *Plutarch,* 117-121.] We may compare the Latin : Habet Deus suas horas, et moras [God has His own times and delays]; and the Spanish : Dios no se queja, mas lo suyo no lo deja [God is not in a hurry, but He forsakes not His purpose.]

† Dii laneos habent pedes.

this proverb ? Indeed, meditating on such and on the source from which we have derived them, one is sometimes tempted to believe that the faith in a divine retribution evermore making itself felt in the world, this sense of a Nemesis, as men used to call it, was stronger and deeper in the earlier and better days of heathendom, than alas ! it is in a sunken Christendom now.

But to resume. Even those proverbs which have acquired an use which seems to unite at once the trivial and the profane, may yet on closer inspection be found to be very far from having either triviality or profaneness cleaving to them. There is one, for instance, often taken lightly enough upon the lips : *Talk of the devil, and he is sure to appear* *; or as it used to be : *Talk of the devil, and his imps will appear ;* or as in German it is : *Paint the devil on the wall, and he will shew himself anon* ;—which yet contains truth serious and important enough, if we would only give heed to it : it contains, in fact, a very solemn warning against a very dangerous sin, I mean, curiosity about evil. It has been often noticed, and is a very curious psychological fact, that there is a tendency in a great crime to reproduce itself, to call forth, that is, other crimes of the same character : and there is a fearful response which the evil we may hear or read about, is in danger of finding in our own hearts. This danger, then,

[* The corresponding adage in Latin was, ' Lupus in fabula', the wolf in the story (which appears when it is mentioned). ' Eccum tibi lupum in sermone ! '— Plautus, *Stichus*, iv. 1, 71. Polydore Vergil, *Proverbia*, 1511, fol. vii.]

assuredly makes it true wisdom, and a piece of moral prudence on the part of all to whom this is permitted, to avoid knowing or learning about the evil ; especially when neither duty nor necessity oblige them thereto. It is men's wisdom to talk as little about the devil, either with themselves or with others, as they can ; lest he appear to them. ' I agree with you', says Niebuhr very profoundly in one of his letters *, ' that it is better not to read books in which you make the acquaintance of the devil.' And certainly there is a remarkable commentary on this proverb, so interpreted, in the earnest warning given to the children of Israel, that they should not so much as *inquire* how the nations which were before them in Canaan, served their gods, with what cruelties, with what abominable impurities, lest through this inquiry they should be themselves entangled in the same. (Deut. xii. 29, 30.) They were not to talk about the devil, lest he should appear to them.

And other proverbs, too, which at first sight may seem over-familiar with the name of the great enemy of mankind, yet contain lessons which it would be an infinite pity to lose ; as this German : *Where the devil cannot come, he will send* † ; a proverb of very serious import, which excellently sets out to us the *penetrative* character of temptations, and the certainty that they will follow and find men out in their secretest retreats. It rebukes the absurdity of supposing that by any outward arrangements, cloistral retirements, flights into the

---

* *Life,* vol. i. p. 312.

† Wo der Teufel nicht hin mag kommen, da send er seinen Boten hin.

wilderness, sin can be kept at a distance. So far
from this, temptations will inevitably overleap all
these outward and merely artificial barriers which
may be raised up against them ; for our great
enemy is as formidable from a seeming distance as
in close combat ; *where he cannot come, he will
send.* There are others of the same family, as the
following : *The devil's meal is half bran ;* or *all
bran,* as the Italians still more boldly proclaim it *;
unrighteous gains are sure to disappoint the getter ;
the pleasures of sin, even in this present time, are
largely dashed with its pains. And this : *He had
need of a long spoon that eats with the devil ;*—
men fancy they can cheat the arch-cheater, can
advance in partnership with him up to a certain
point, and then, whenever the connexion becomes
too dangerous, break it off at their will ; being sure
in this to be miserably deceived ; for, to quote
another in the same tone : *He who has shipped
the devil, must carry him over the water.* Granting
these and the like to have been often carelessly
uttered, yet they all rest upon a true moral basis
in the main. This last series of proverbs I will
close with an Arabic one, to which not even this
appearance of levity can be ascribed ; for it is as
solemn and sublime in form as it is profoundly deep
in substance : *The blessings of the evil Genii are
curses.* How deep a meaning the story of Fortunatus acquires, when taken as a commentary on this.

But I am warned to draw my lecture to an end.
I have adduced in the course of these lectures
no inconsiderable number of proverbs, and have
sought for the most part to deduce from them

* La farina del diavolo se ne và in semola.

lessons, which were lessons in common for us all. There is one, however, which I must not pass over, for I feel that it contains an especial lesson for myself, and a lesson which I should do wisely and well at this present time to lay to heart. When the Spaniards would describe a tedious writer, one who possesses the art of exhausting the patience of his readers, they say of him : *He leaves nothing in his inkstand.* The phrase is a singularly happy one, for assuredly there is no such secret of tediousness, no such certain means of wearing out the attention of our readers or our hearers, as the attempt to say everything ourselves, instead of leaving something to be filled up by their intelligence ; while the merits of a composition are often displayed as really, if not so prominently, in what is passed over as in what is set down ; in nothing more than in the just measure of the confidence which it shows in the capacities and powers of those to whom it is addressed. I would not willingly come under the condemnation, which waits on them who thus *leave nothing in their inkstand ;* and lest I should do so, I will bring now this my final lecture to its close, and ask you to draw out for yourselves those further lessons from proverbs, which I am sure they are abundantly capable of yielding.

APPENDIX

ON THE METRICAL LATIN PROVERBS OF THE MIDDLE AGES. (See p. 27.)

I HAVE not seen anywhere brought together a collection of these medieval proverbs cast into the form of a rhyming hexameter. Erasmus, though he often illustrates the proverbs of the ancient world by those of the new, does not quote, as far as I am aware, through the whole of his enormous collection, a single one of these which occupy a middle place between the two ; a fact which in its way is curiously illustrative of the degree to which the attention of the great Humanists at the revival of learning was exclusively directed to the classical literature of Greece and Rome. Yet proverbs in this form exist in considerable number, being of very various degrees of merit, as will be seen from the following selection ; in which some are keen and piquant enough, while others are of very subordinate value ; those which seemed to me utterly valueless—and they were not few—I have excluded altogether. The reader familiar with proverbs will detect correspondents to very many of them, besides the few which I have quoted, in one modern language or another, often in many.

Accipe, sume, cape, tria sunt gratissima Papæ.
[Receive, take, seize are the three words the Pope
likes best.]

> Let me observe here, once for all, that the length-
> ening of the final syllable in *capē*, is not to be set
> down to the ignorance or carelessness of the writer ;
> but in the theory of the medieval hexameter, the
> unavoidable stress or pause on the first syllable
> of the third foot was counted sufficient to lengthen
> the shortest syllable in that position.

Ad secreta poli curas extendere noli.
[Let not thy curiosity extend to the secrets of
heaven.]

Ægro sanato, frustra dices, Numerato.
[When the sickman is cured it is in vain to say,
Pay.]

Amphora sub veste raro portatur honeste.
[A vessel hidden under the cloak is seldom come
by honestly.]

Ante Dei vultum nihil unquam restat inultum.
[In God's sight nothing ever remains unavenged.]

Ante molam primus qui venit, non molat imus.
[He who comes first to the mill must not grind
last.]

> A rule of natural equity : Prior tempore, prior jure ;
> —*First come, first serve.*—' Whoso first cometh to
> the mill, first grint'.—*Chaucer.*

Arbor naturam dat fructibus atque figuram.
[The kind of fruit and its form depend on the
tree.]

Arbor ut ex fructu, sic nequam noscitur actu.
[As a tree is known by its fruit so a knave by his
deeds.]

Ars compensabit quod vis tibi magna negabit.

[Skill will make up to thee what mere strength will
 deny.]
Artem natura superat sine vi, sine curâ.
[Nature surpasses art without effort or anxiety.]
Aspera vox, Ite, sed vox est blanda, Venite.
[' Go ' is a stern word, but ' come ' persuasive.]

> An allusion to Matt. xxv. 34, 41. [Rather, example
> is better than command.]

Cari rixantur, rixantes conciliantur.
[Lovers quarrel and straightway make it up.]
Carius est carum, si prægustatur amarum.
[The dear is all the dearer for tasting bitter at
 first.]
Casus dementis correctio fit sapientis.
[The fool's downfall is the wise man's correction.]
Catus sæpe satur cum capto mure jocatur.
[The cat when she's full often plays with the mouse.]
Cautus homo cavit, si quem natura notavit.
[When nature has set her mark on him the careful
 man is ware of him.]
Conjugium sine prole, dies veluti sine sole.
[Marriage without children is like a day without
 sunshine.]
Contra vim mortis non herbula crescit in hortis.
[There's no herb growing in the garden that's
 good against death.]
Cui puer assuescit, major dimittere nescit.
[What the child is accustomed to he won't let go
 when he is old.]

> The same appears also in a pentameter, and under
> an Horatian image : Quod nova testa capit, in-
> veterata sapit. [What a jar holds when it is new it
> smacks of when it is old.]

Cui sunt multa bona, huic dantur plurima dona.
[He who has much gets many a gift.]
Cum jocus est verus, jocus est malus atque severus.
[A joke that is true is sharp and shrewd.]

> So the Spanish : Malas son las burlas verdaderas
> [Scottish : A true bourd is nae bourd.]

Curvum se præbet quod in uncum crescere debet.
[What is growing to be a crook must needs be
crooked.]
Curia Romana non quærit ovem sine lanâ.
[The Court of Rome doesn't want the sheep with-
out its wool.]
Dat bene, dat multum, qui dat cum munere vultum.
[He is a good and bountiful giver who gives a smile
with his gift.]

> 'He that sheweth mercy, with cheerfulness.'
> (Rom. xii. 8.) Cf. Ecclus. xxxv. 9 ; Seneca, *De
> Benef.* i. 1.

Deficit ambobus qui vult servire duobus.
[He who tries to serve two masters serves neither.]
Dormit secure, cui non est functio curæ.
[He who has no anxieties sleeps soundly.]

> *Far from court, far from care.*

Ebibe vas totum, si vis cognoscere potum.
[Drink up the whole draught if you want to know
what it is.]
Est facies testis, quales intrinsecus estis.
[The face shows what you are inwardly.]
Est nulli certum cui pugna velit dare sertum.
[None for certain can know how the battle
will go.]
Ex linguâ stultâ veniunt incommoda multa.
[Many troubles have sprung from a foolish tongue.]

Ex minimo crescit, sed non cito fama quiescit.
[Report has a small beginning but lasts long.]
Fœmina ridendo flendo fallitque canendo.
[Woman beguiles with tears, singing and smiles.]
Frangitur ira gravis, cum fit responsio suavis.
[A soft answer disarms wrath of its violence.]
Fures in lite pandunt abscondita vitæ.
[Thieves discover their secrets when they come into
    court.]

> So in Spanish : Riñen las comadres, y dicense las
> verdades. [When gossips fall out they tell the truth.]

Furtivus potus plenus dulcedine totus.
[A stolen draught is ever the sweetest.]
Hoc retine verbum, frangit Deus omne superbum.
[Remember this saying, God crushes all pride.]
Illa mihi patria est, ubi pascor, non ubi nascor.
[Where I get my living, not where I am born, is
    my true country.]
Impedit omne forum defectus denariorum.
[Want of cash spoils all marketing.]
In vestimentis non stat sapientia mentis.
[Wisdom does not depend on one's garb.]
In vili veste nemo tractatur honeste.
[No one in poor clothing is honourably entreated.]

> The Russians have a worthier proverb : *A man's
> reception is according to his coat ; his dismissal ac-
> cording to his sense.*

Linguam frænare plus est quam castra domare.
[Curbing the tongue is greater than taking a strong-
    hold.]
Lingua susurronis est pejor felle draconis.
[The tongue of the whisperer is worse than serpent's
    poison.]

Musca, canes, mimi veniunt ad fercula primi.
[Flies and dogs and jesters are the first to come
    to meat.]
Mus salit in stratum, cum scit non adfore catum.
[The mouse springs on the couch when it knows
    the cat's not there.]
Ne credas undam placidam non esse profundam.
[Think not that the water is not deep because it
    is still.]
Nil cito mutabis donec meliora parabis,
[Change nothing in a hurry till you get what's
    better.]
Nobilitas morum plus ornat quam genitorum.
[Nobleness of character adorns more than that of
    ancestors.]
Non colit arva bene, qui semen mandat arenæ.
[He's not a good farmer who sows on the sand.]
Non est in mundo dives qui dicit, Abundo.
[There's not a rich man in the world who says
    ' I have enough'.]
Non habet anguillam, per caudam qui tenet illam.
[He hasn't got the eel who holds it by the tail.]
Non stat securus, qui protinus est ruiturus.
[He who is on the way to ruin does not stand safe.]
Non vult scire satur quid jejunus patiatur.
[He who has a full stomach doesn't want to
    know what the empty one suffers.]
Omnibus est nomen, sed idem non omnibus omen.
[All have names but few fulfil their meaning.]

> In a world of absolute truth, every name would be
> the exact utterance of the thing or person that bore
> it ; but in our world not every Irenæus is peace-
> able, nor every Blanche a blonde. Vigilantius
> ought rather, according to Jerome, to have been
> named Dormitantius ; and Antiochus Epiphanes,

(the Illustrious,) was for the Jews Antiochus
Epimanes, (the Insane.)

Parvis imbutus tentabis grandia tutus.
[With small ambitions you may essay great things
safely.]
Pelle sub agninâ latitat mens sæpe lupina.
[Under the sheep's fleece often lurks a wolfish
disposition.]
Per multum, Cras, Cras, omnis consumitur ætas.
[In ' to-morrow and to-morrow ' a whole life is
wasted.]
Prodigus est natus de parco patre creatus.
[From a thrifty father is born a spendthrift son.]
Quando tumet venter, produntur facta latenter.
[When the stomach is full secrets are betrayed.]
Qui bene vult fari, debet bene præmeditari.
[He who would speak well must think it over before-
hand.]
Quidquid agit mundus, monachus vult esse secun-
dus.
[However the world wags the monk means to
prosper.]
Qui petit alta nimis, retro lapsus ponitur imis.
[He who aims too high sinks back among the
lowest.]
Qui pingit florem non pingit floris odorem.
[You may paint the flower, but you can't paint
its scent.]
Qui se non noscat, vicini jurgia poscat.
[If one know not himself let him provoke the
abuse of his neighbour.]
Quisquis amat luscam, luscam putat esse venus-
tam.
[Whoever loves a plain lass thinks her a beauty.]

Quisquis amat ranam, ranam putat esse Dianam.
[If one is in love with a frog he thinks it a god-
    dess.]
Quod raro cernit oculi lux, cor cito spernit.
[What the eye seldom sees the heart soon slights.]
Quo minime reris, de gurgite pisce frueris.
[You will get a fish from the stream when you least
    expect it.]
Quos vult sors ditat, et quos vult sub pede tritat.
[Fate enriches whom she will and crushes whom
    she will.]
Res satis est nota, plus fœtent stercora mota.
[Everybody knows that the dunghill stinks worst
    when it's stirred.]
Scribatur portis, Meretrix est janua mortis.
[Let it be written on her gates, a harlot is the
    gate of death.]
Sepes calcatur, quâ pronior esse putatur.
[The hedge is trodden down where it seems to be
    lowest.]
Si curiam curas, pariet tibi curia curas.
[If you care for the courts, the courts will provide
    you with cares.]
Si nequeas plures, vel te solummodo cures.
[Care for yourself at least if you can't for others.]
Si non morderis, cane quid latrante vereris ?
[Why are you afraid of the dogs barking since
    you are not bitten ?]
Stare diu nescit, quod non aliquando quiescit.
[That can't stand long which never takes rest.]
Subtrahe ligna focis, flammam restinguere si vis.
[If you would quench the fire take off the fuel.]
Sunt asini multi solum bino pede fulti.
[There's many an ass that walks on two feet.]

Sus magis in cœno gaudet quam fonte sereno.
[The sow delights more in mire than clear water.]
Tam male nil cusum, quod nullum prosit in usum.
[Nothing is so badly forged but it's good for some-
    thing.]
Totâ equidem novi plus testâ pars valet ovi.
[A bit of the egg, say I, is worth more than the
    whole of the shell.]
Ultra posse viri non vult Deus ulla requiri.
[God never means to ask anything beyond a man's
    power.]
Verba satis celant mores, eademque revelant.
[Words serve to hide one's character as well as
    show it.]
Vos inopes nostis, quis amicus quisve sit hostis.
[When you become poor you know who is your
    friend and who your enemy.]
Vulpes vult fraudem, lupus agnum, fœmina
    laudem.
[The fox likes tricks, the wolf lamb, a woman
    praise.]

Add to these a few of the same description, but
unrhymed :

Catus amat pisces, sed non vult tingere plantam.
[The cat loves fish, but doesn't like to wet her feet.]

> It is with this proverb, which is almost of all
> languages, that Lady Macbeth taunts her husband,
> as one—
> 'Letting "I dare not" wait upon "I would,"
> Like the poor cat i' the adage'.—Act I. Scene 7.*

[* This adage is quoted in *Pierce the Ploughman's
Crede* (ab. 1394) :
    'Thou woldest not weten thy fote and woldest fich
    kacchen' (l. 405).]

Cochlea consiliis, in factis esto volucris.
[Be a snail in forming your plans, a bird in carry-
ing them into action.]
Dat Deus omne bonum, sed non per cornua taurum.
[God gives every blessing, but not a bull by the
horns.]

> The Chinese say : *Even the ripest fruit does not drop
> into one's mouth ;* and another Latin : Non volat
> in buccas assa columba tuas. [Roasted pigeon
> doesn't fly into your jaws.]

Ense cadunt multi, perimit sed crapula plures.
[Many perish by the sword, but more through
drink.]
Furfure se miscens porcorum dentibus estur.
[He who mixes himself up with draff gets eaten
by pigs.]

> With a slight variation the Italian : Chi si fa
> fango, il porco lo calpesta. [He who makes him-
> self dirt is trampled on by swine.]

Ipsa dies quandoque parens, quandoque noverca.
[The same day is sometimes a mother, sometimes
a step-mother.]
Invidus haud eadem semper quatit ostia Dæmon.
[Envious Fate does not always knock at the same
door.]
Mirari, non rimari, sapientia vera est.
[To admire without rifling is true wisdom.]
Nomina si nescis, perit et cognitio rerum.]
[Knowledge of things is gone if you know not
their names.]
Non stillant omnes quas cernis in aëre nubes.
[All the clouds you see don't turn to rain.]
Non venit ad silvam, qui cuncta rubeta veretur.

[He who is afraid of every bramble will never come
to the wood.]

Occurrit cuicunque Deus, paucique salutant.

[God meets every man, but few recognise Him.]

Pro ratione Deus dispertit frigora vestis.

[God gives us cold according to our clothing.]

Quod rarum carum ; vilescit quotidianum.

[What is scarce is valued ; while everyday things
are held cheap.]

Sermones blandi non radunt ora loquentis.

[Smooth discourses don't roughen the lips of the
speaker.]

Stultorum calami carbones, mœnia chartæ.

[Charcoal is the pen of fools, and walls their paper.]

> So the French : Muraille blanche, papier des sots
> · [A white wall fools' paper.]

Add further a few which occupy two lines :

Argue consultum, te diliget ; argue stultum,
Avertet vultum, nec te dimittet inultum.

[Confute a wiseman and he'll love thee ; confute
a fool
He will turn away his face and not suffer thee to
go unpunished.]

Balnea cornici non prosunt, nec meretrici ;
Nec meretrix munda, nec cornix alba fit undâ

[Washing is no good for a crow nor a harlot :
Water can't make the one white or the other clean.]

Dives eram dudum ; fecerunt me tria nudum ;
Alea, vina, Venus ; tribus his sum factus egenus.

[Once I was rich, but three things left me bare ;
Dice, wine, and women; by these three came I poor.]

Quando mulcetur villanus, pejor habetur ;
Ungentem pungit, pungentem rusticus ungit.

[When a boor is cockered he becomes worse than
　　before ;
The clown stabs him who butters him, and butters
　　him who stabs him.]

> Latin medieval ones in the same spirit abound :
> among others this detestable one with its curious
> triple rhyme : Rustica gens est optima flens, et
> pessima ridens. [The clownish sort are best when
> in grief, worst when they are merry.]

Si bene barbatum faceret sua barba beatum,
Nullus in hoc circo queat esse beatior hirco.
[If a big beard would make the bearded happy,
None on this earth should be so happy as the
　　he-goat.]
Si quâ sede sedes, et sit tibi commoda sedes,
Illâ sede sede, nec ab illâ sede recede.
[If you find your seat to your mind where you
　　happen to be sitting,
Keep sitting on that seat and withdraw not there-
　　from.]
Hoc scio pro certo, quod si cum stercore certo,
　　Vinco seu vincor, semper ego maculor.
[Of this I am sure, that if I fight with a sweep
　　(lit. dung)
Whether I come off first or second-best I get
　　besmirched.*]
Multum deliro, si cuique placere requiro ;
　　Omnia qui potuit, hâc sine dote fuit.
[I am mad indeed, if I seek to please everybody ;
He who could do everything could not do this.]
Permutant mores homines, cum dantur honores ;
　　Corde stat inflato pauper, honore dato.

[* Compare the Spanish : El golpe de la sarten, aunque
no duele, tizna. (The blow of a frying-pan smuts if it
does not hurt).]

[Men change their characters when honours are
   bestowed on them ;
The poor man is puffed up with pride when honours
   come to him.]

APPENDIX, NOTE A (P. 2)

'The Precepts of Ptah-hotep' about 3440 B.C.,
preserved in the Papyrus Prisse, ' the oldest book
in the world, ' profess to be founded on the
wisdom of authorities still more ancient, and to
give ' the words of those who have heard the
counsels of former days ' (see *Records of the Past*,
N.S. iii, 16 *seq.*) ; among them are the following :

' Good words are scarcer than emeralds '.

' Thou hast the advantage of the angry if thou
keepest silence '.

' The impassive man is the better of the two '.

' He that is wrong fights against himself '.

' He is to blame who makes a bad use of his
moments'.

' Listen with kindness if you would have a clear
explanation '.

' Thousands ruin themselves for a moment's
enjoyment '.

' The great man is the steward of God's goods '.

' A wife will be doubly attached if her chain is
pleasant '.

' A good listener is a good speaker '.

' A son who receives his father's instruction will
grow old '.

' The wisdom of a son is his docility '.

' Let thy thoughts be free, but thy mouth restrained '.

' A good son is a gift of God '.

' Keep a cheerful countenance as long as life lasts '.

Other Precepts of Ptah-hotep are :

' God's doings are unknown '.

' If thou wouldest be wise make thy son pleasing to God '.

' What God loves is obedience, what He hates is disobedience '.

' A good son is one of the gifts of God '.

Among the ' Maxims of Ani ' are :

' What God's house hates is much speaking '.

' God will judge the right '.

' Whoso magnifieth God, He magnifieth '.

See Budge, *Book of the Dead*, 1895, pp. lxxxv–lxxxviii.

Several maxims which appear to be popular proverbs are quoted from ' The Moral Papyrus of Boulaq' :

' He who hates idleness will come without being called '.

' A good walker comes to his journey's end without needing to hasten '.

' The ox which goes at the head of the herd and leads the others to pasture is but an animal like his fellows '.

See Maspero, *The Struggle of the Nations*, p. 503.

APPENDIX, NOTE B (P. 27)

The following ' Proverbs of Alfred ' are taken from a thirteenth century MS. printed in Dr.

Morris's *Old English Miscellany* (Early English Text Society, 1872), pp. 102 *seq.*, where they are attributed to ' Alfred Englene derling '.

1. ' Hwych so [what so] the mon soweth.
   Al swuch he schal mowe.
   And eueruyches monnes dom
   to his owere dure churreth ' [own door returneth]. ll. 82–5.

2. ' Hi that nule one youhthe [will not in youth]
   Yeorne leorny [diligently learn] . . .
   that him schal on elde
   sore rewe '. ll. 106–11.

3. ' Hwhat is gold bute ston
   bute if hit haueth wismon ' [unless a wise-man has it]. ll. 131–2.

4. ' Strong [hard] hit is to reowe [row]
   a-yeyn the see that floweth,
   so hit is to swynke [labour]
   a-yeyn vnylimpe ' [misfortune]. ll. 145–8

5. ' Monymon weneth [expects]
   that he wene ne tharf [what he need not expect]
   longes lyues ' [length of life]. ll. 160–2.

6. ' Nys no wrt uexynde [there is no plant growing]
   a wude ne a velde [in wood nor in field]
   that euer muwe thas feye [may the death-doomed]
   furth vp-holde ' [maintain in life]. ll. 168–171.

7. ' Ayhte nys non ildre istreon [Property is not fore-bears' gain].
   ac hit is Godes lone '. ll. 185–6.

8. ' Monymon for his gold
   haueth Godes vrre [wrath]. ll. 204–5.
10. ' Ne schal-tu neuere thi wife
    by hire wlyte [face] cheose'. ll. 248–9.
11. ' Monymon singeth
    that wif hom bringeth,
    wiste he hwat he brouhte
    wepen he myhte'. ll. 264–7.
12. ' Ne wurth [be] thu neuer so wod [mad]
    nee so wyn-drunke
    that euere segge [tell] thine wife
    alle thine wille'. ll. 269–72.
13. ' Wymmon is word-woth [word-mad]
    and haueth tunge to [too] swift'. ll.
    281–2.
14. ' Ofte museth [mouseth] the kat
    after hire moder'. ll. 296–7.
15. ' Selde wurth he blythe and gled
    the mon that is his wiues qued'. [scorn].
    ll. 304–5.
16. ' Mony appel is bryht with-vte
    and bitter with-inne,
    So is mony wymmon
    on hyre fader bure' [father's chamber].
    ll. 306–9.
17. ' Wymmon wepeth for mod [mood]
    oftere than for eny god' [good]. ll. 323–4.
18. ' Hit is ifurn iseyd [long ago said]
    that cold red [rede, counsel] is quene
    [woman's] red'. ll. 335–6.
19. ' At chepynge and at chyreche [market and
    church]
    freond thu the iwurche' [make thee friends].
    ll. 373–4.

20. ' Mid [with] fewe worde wismon
fele biluken wel con ' [much can comprise
well]. ll. 419–20.
21. ' Sottes [fool's] bolt is sone i-scohte ' [shot].
l. 421.
22. ' Ofte tunge breketh bon,
theyh [though] heo seolf nabbe non '. ll.
424–5.
23. ' Wis child is fader [father's] blisse '. l.
428.
24. ' Betere is child vnbore
thane vnbuhsum ' [disobedient]. l. 450.
25. ' Wurthu [Be thou] never so wod [mad]
ne so desi [silly] of thi mod
thad evere sige [tell] thi frend
al that the [thee] likit
ne al the thonkes [seems] '. ll. 478–82.
26. ' Elde [Age] cumid to tune [town]
mid fele unkethe costes ' [many strange
habits]. ll. 534–5.
27. ' He that is ute bi-loken [shut out of doors]
he is innu sone forgeten '. ll. 554–5.
28. ' Wrthe thad z-wurthe [Be what may be]
i-wurthe Godes will ' [God's will is done].
ll. 571–2.
29. ' Leue [beloved] sone dere,
ne ches thee neuere to fere [for a companion]
littele mon, ne long, ne red
yif thu wld don after mi red ' [counsel].
ll. 677–80.

Appendix, Note C (p. 27)

Another exemplification of the proverbial philosophy of the thirteenth century is presented in the Proverbs of Hendyng, which have often been printed. Hendyng, from Old English *hende*, clever, sly, seems to have been a popular personification of sagacity and shrewdness. The text here used is taken from K. Boddeker, *Altenglischie Dichtungen des MS. Harl* 2253, pp. 285–300.

‘ God [good] beginning maketh god endynge
 Quoth Hendyng ’ *. l. 14.

‘ Wyt and wysdom is god warysoun ’ [protection]. l. 21.

‘ Ase fele thede ase feli thewes ’. l. 29.
[So many people so many customs.]

‘ Luef child lore byhoueth ’. l. 37.
[A loved child requires teaching.]

‘ Whoso yong lereth, olt he ne leseth ’ [loseth]. l. 45.

‘ Let lust over gon, eft [later] hit shal the lyke ’ [thee please]. l. 53.

‘ Betere is eye sor then al blynd.’ l. 61.

‘ Sely [innocent] child is sone ylered ’ [taught]. l. 69.

‘ Wel fyht that wel flyth ’. l. 77.
[He fights well that flies well.]

Compare :

   ‘ Those that fly may fight again
    Which he can never do that’s slain ’.
      Butler, *Hudibras*, pt. 3, cant. 3. l. 243.

‘ That same man that renneth awaie,
 Maie again fight another daie ’.
      1542, N. Udall, *Apophthegmes of Erasmus,*
       p. 372 (ed. Roberts).

---

* Every proverb has this addition.

' Sottes bolt is sone shote '. 1. 85.

' Tel thou neuer thy fo that thy fot aketh '. 1. 93.

Betere is appel ygeve then y-ete.

[An apple given is better than eaten.]

' Este bueth oune brondes '. 1. 109.

[Pleasant are one's own brands, i.e. fireside.]

' Gredy is the godless '. 1. 117.

' When the coppe [cup] is follest, thenne ber hire feyrest '. 1. 125.

' Tonge breketh bon and nath hire selue non '. 1. 144.

' That me lutel geueth he my lyf ys on '. 1. 152.

[He that giveth me little wishes me to live.]

' The bet the be the bet the byse '. 1. 160.

[The better it is with thee the better take heed to thee.]

' Vnder boske [bush] shal men weder abide '. 1. 168.

' When the bale is hest thenne is the bote nest '. 1. 176.

[When the evil is highest the boot (help) is nighest.]

' Brend child fur dredeth '. 1. 184.

[A burnt child dreadeth fire.]

' Selde cometh lone lahynde hom '. 1. 192.

[Seldom loan comes laughing home.]

' Owen ys owen, and other mennes eduiteth '. 1. 200.

[One's own is one's own, and twitteth (condemns) other men's.]

' Fer from eghe fer from herte '. 1. 208.

[Compare, ' Out of sight out of mind.']

' Of unboht hude men kerveth brod thongs '. 1. 216.

[From an unbought hide men cut broad thongs].*

' He is fre of hors that ner nade non '. l. 224.

[He that never had a horse is ready to lend it.]

' Lyht chep luthere yeldes ' l. 232.

[A thoughtless purchase turns out badly.]

' Dere is boht the hony that is licked of the thorne '. l. 240.

' Wel abit that wel may tholye '. l. 248.

[He well abides who well can suffer.]

' Ofte rap [haste] reweth '. l. 256.

' Of alle mester men mest me hongeth theues '. l. 264.

[Of all kinds of men the most hanged are thieves.]

' Euer out cometh euel sponne web '. l. 272.

[Evil always comes out when the web is spun.]

' Monimon for londe wyueth to shonde ' [shame]. l. 280.

' Ffrendles ys the dede '. l. 288.

[The dead have no friends.]

' Drynk eft lasse and go by lyhte hom '. l. 296.

[Drink less in future and go home while 'tis light.]

' Hope of long lyf gyleth mony god wyf '. l. 304.

* ' Men cut large thongs of other men's lether ' occurs in *The Paston Letters*, ab. 1260, vol. ii. p. 226.

SELECT BIBLIOGRAPHY

GENERAL

Bibliography.

Gratet-Duplessis, P. A., *Bibliographie parémiologique. Études bibliographiques sur les ouvrages consacrés aux Proverbes dans toutes les langues.* Paris, 1847.

Nopitsch, C. C., *Literatur du Sprichwörter.* Nurnberg, 1822.

Stirling Maxwell, Sir W., *An Essay towards a collection of books relating to Proverbs, Emblems, etc., at Keir.* London, 1860.

Collections.

Bohn, H. G., *A Handbook of Proverbs.* 1857.

Bohn, H. G., *A Polyglot of Foreign Proverbs.* 1857.

Christy, R., *Proverbs, Maxims and Phrases of all Ages,* 2 vols. London, 1888.

Dennys, E. M., *Proverbs of many Nations.* London, 1890.

Fielding, T., *Select Proverbs of all Nations.* 1824.

Hulme, F. E., *Proverb Lore.* 1902.

Kelly, W. W., *Proverbs of All Nations.* N.D.

Lean, V. S., *Collectanea, Proverbs, etc.* 5 vols. 1904.

Mawr, E. B., *Analogous Proverbs in Ten Languages.* 1882.

Middlemore, J., *Proverbs in Various Languages.* London, 1889.

Proverbs, or the Manual of Wisdom : the best English, Spanish, French, Italian Proverbs, Wise Sayings, Precepts, etc. Oxford, 1803.

Ward, C., *National Proverbs in the principal languages of Europe.* London, 1842.

ENGLAND ;

Arthur, S. K., *A Bouquet of Brevities : a selection of Maxims, Proverbs and Sayings.*

Belcour, G., *English Proverbs (and their French Equivalents).*

Bellezza, P., *Proverbi Inglisi, Studio Comparativo.* Milano, 1893.

Bland, R., *Proverbs chiefly taken from the Adagia of Erasmus with explanations and examples from the Spanish, Italian, French and English Languages.* 2 vols. 1814.

Bolton, C. E., *Popular Proverbs.* 1882.

Bourdillon, F., *The Voice of the People : Proverbs examined and applied.* London, 1896.

Camden, W., *Remaines concerning Britaine.* 1637. (*Proverbs*, pp. 289–310.)

Carminum Proverbialium totius humanæ vitæ statum breviter delineantium loci communes. Edinburgh, 1701.

The Crossing [= contradiction] *of Proverbs.* 1616.

Dykes, O., *English Proverbs, with moral Reflections.* 1709.

Fuller, T., *Gnomologia, Adagies and Proverbs.* 2 vols. 1728–31.

Gainsford, Thomas, *Rich Cabinet.* 1616. [*Has some old proverbs.*]

Gomme, G. L., *Gentleman's Magazine : Dialect, Proverbs, Word-lore.*

Haeckel, *Das Sprichwort bei Chaucer.*

Hazlitt, W. C., *English Proverbs and Proverbial Phrases.* 1868.

H[erbert], G., *Outlandish Proverbs.* 1640. (2nd ed. *Jacula Prudentum*).

Heywood, J., *A Dialogue conteyning the number of effectual Proverbes,* etc. 1546.

—— *Two hundred epigrammes upon* 200 *Proverbes, with a thyrde hundred newely added.* 1555.

Hood, E. P., *The World of Proverb.* London, 1885.

Hoole, C., *Cato's Distichs concerning Manners—Publius'*

Stage Verses or *Seneca's Proverbs in Latin and English.* 1727.

Howell, J., *Proverbs or Old Sayed Saws and Adages.* 1659.

Kellner, L., *Altenglische Spruchweisheit.* Wien, 1897.

Mair, J., *Handbook of Proverbs, English, Scottish, Irish, etc.* 1874.

Mair, J. A., *Proverbs and Family Mottoes.* London, 1891.

Mapletoft, J., *Select Proverbs.* 1707.

Palmer, S., *Moral Essays on English, Scotch and Foreign Proverbs.* 1710.

Proverbs of Alfred (xiii. cent.) [in Morris, *Old Eng. Miscellany,* E.E.T.S., pp. 102–138].

Ray, J., *A Collection of English Proverbs, etc.* 1670.

Rees, F. A., *Practical Points in Popular Proverbs.*

Taverner, R., *The Garden of Wysdome, Proverbs, etc.* 1539.

Taverner, R., *Proverbes and Adagies gathered out of the Chiliades of Erasmus, with newe additions as well of Latyn proverbes as of Englysshe.* 1545.

Tricomi, G., *Handbook of English Proverbs.* Catania, 1900.

"Wren, J.," *Old Proverbs with New Faces.* 1893.

Special.

Cowan, F., *Dictionary of Proverbs relating to the Sea.* Greenesburgh, 1894.

Cheales, A. B., *Proverbial Folk-lore.* Dorking, N.D.

Denham, M. A., *Collection of Proverbs and Popular Sayings relating to the Seasons, Weather, etc.* (Percy Soc.), 1846.

Henderson, G., *Popular Rhymes, Sayings and Proverbs of the County of Berwick.* Newcastle-on-Tyne, 1856.

Inwards, Richard, *A Collection of Proverbs, Sayings and Rules concerning the Weather.* 1893.

Markham, Christopher A., *The Proverbs of Northamptonshire.*

Swainson, C., *Handbook of Weather Folk-lore, Proverbial Sayings, etc.* Edinburgh, 1873.

Scotland.

Cheviot, A., *Proverbial Expressions, etc., of Scotland.* 1896.

Hislop, A., *The Proverbs of Scotland.* Edinburgh (no date).

Kelly, J., *Collection of Scottish Proverbs.* 1721.

M., M. L., *Scottish Proverbs.* Arbroath, 1895.

Macintosh, D., *A Collection of Gaelic Proverbs.* Edinburgh, 1882.

Maclean, M., *Literature of the Highlands,* 1904 (Gaelic Proverbs).

Nicolson, A., *Gaelic Proverbs.* 1880.

Ramsay, A., *Scots Proverbs.* 1797.

Wales.

Richards, T., *Dictionary, Antiquæ Linguæ Britannicæ Thesaurus, being a British, or Welsh-English Dictionary, with a Collection of Proverbs.* Bristol, 1753.

Salisbury, W., *Synwyr Pen pob Kymro : A Collection of Proverbs.* About 1547. Edited by J. G. Evans.

Vaughan, H. H., *British Reason in English Rhyme. Collection of Welsh Proverbs.* London, 1889.

Cregeen, A., *Dictionary of the Manks Language, with Gaelic Proverbs.* Douglas, 1835.

Harrison, W., *Mona Miscellany ; a Selection of Proverbs, Sayings, etc., peculiar to the Isle of Man.* 1869.

Ireland.

Hogan, E., *Irish Proverbs.* 1895 (?).

Wilde Lady, *Ancient Cures, Charms and Usages of Ireland, with a Collection of Irish Proverbs.*

Cornwall.

Lach-Szyrma, W. S., *Cornish Proverbs (Trans. of the Penzance Nat. Hist. and Antiq. Soc.,* 1882–3).

GERMANY

Barten, J., *A Collection of English and German Proverbs.* Hamburgh, 1896.

Borchardt, W., *Die Sprichwörtlichen Redensarten im deutschen Volksmund.* Leipzig, 1888.

Eckart, R., *Stand und Beruf im Volksmund. Eine Sammlung von Sprichwörtern.* Göttingen, 1900.

Eiselein, J., *Sprichwoerter u. Sinnreden d. deutschen Volkes in alter u. neuer Zeit.* Donauoesch. 1838.

Eiselein, J., *Reimhaften, anklingenden, etc. Formeln du hochdeutschen Sprache.* Belle Vue, 1841.

Eisenhart, J. F., *Grundsätze du deutschen Richte Spruchwörtern durch Ammerkungen erläutert.* Leipzig, 1792.

Kirchhofer, M., *Wahrheit u. Dichtung. Sammlung schweizer. Spruechwoerter.* Zuerich, 1824.

Marbach, G. O., *Sprichwörter und Spruchreden der Deutschen.* Leipzig, 1847.

Mühlhause, E., *Die urreligion du deutschen Volkes in hessischen Sitten, Sprüchwörtern, etc.* Cassel, 1860.

Mylius, C. F., *Aus Volkes Mund; Sprichwörtliche Redensarten, etc.* Frankfurt, 1878.

Peter, A., *Volksthümliches aus Oesterreichisch-Schlesien.* 2 vols. (*Sprichwörte,* vol. 1). Troppau, 1865-7.

Reinsberg-Düringsfeld, O. F. v., *Das Wetter im Sprüchwort.* Leipzig, 1864.

Reinsberg-Düringsfeld, O. F. v., *Die Frau im Sprichwort.* Leipzig, 1862.

Sandvoss, F., *So spricht das Volk.* Berlin, 1860.

Simrock, C. J., *Die deutschen Sprichwörter.* Basel, 1888.

Spruechwoerter u. Redensarten, 6000 deutsche, hrsg. v. J. M. Braun. Stuttgart, 1804.

Steiger, K., *Pretiosen deutschen Sprichwörter.* St. Gallen, 1865.

Tappius, E., *Germanicorum adagiorum cum latinis ac græcis collatorum centuriae septem.* Argentinæ, 1539.

Wagner, K., *Sprichwörter und Redensarten in Rudolstadt.* Rudolstadt, 1882.

Wander, *Deutsches Sprichwörter Lexicon.* 1869.

Zacher, J., *Die deutschen Sprichwoertersammlungen nebst Beitr. z. Characteristik d. Meusebachschen Bibliothek.* Leipzig, 1852.

Zincgref, J. W., *Scharfsinnige Sprueche d. Teutschen, Apophthegmata genannt.* Mannheim, 1835.

Zounder, *Deutsche Sprach Wörterbuch.*

Belgium and Holland.

Eckart, R., *Niederdeutsche Sprichwörter.* Braunschweig, 1893.

Harrebomée, J., *Spreekwoordenboek der nederlandsche taal.* 3 vols. Utrecht, 1853-64.

Stoett, F. A., *Nederlandsche Sprukwoorden*. Zutphen, 1900.

Dirksen, C., *Ostfriesische Sprichwörter*. Ruhrort, 1889–91.

FRANCE

Belcour, G., *Selection of French Proverbs*. London, 1882.

———— *English Proverbs and French Equivalents*.

Bellingen, Fleury de, *Explication de Proverbes François*, La Haye, 1656 (also known as *Les Illustres Proverbes Historiques*).

Cahier, P. Ch., *Quelque Six Mille Proverbes et Aphorismes usuels* [*in thirteen languages*]—*Axiomes, ou Formules Scientifiques* [*in Latin*]. Paris, 1856.

Crapelet, G. A., *Proverbes et Dictons Populaires*. Paris, 1831.

De Lincy, le R., *Livre des Proverbes Français*. 2 vols. 1859. (*Bibliographie des Proverbes*, tom ii. pp. 547–596.)

De Méry, M. C., *Histoire Générale des Proverbes, Adages, etc.* 3 vols. 1828.

Dictionnaire des Proverbes Français avec explication Allemande, Latine et Polonaise. Warsaw, 1782.

Duplessis, G., *La Fleur des Proverbes Français*. Paris, 1851.

Lagniet, Jacques, *Recueil des plus illustres proverbes*, Paris, 1657.

Larchey, L., *Nos vieux Proverbs*. Paris, 1886.

Leclercq, T., *Proverbes Dramatiques*. 4 vols. Paris, N.D.

Le Gai, H. [Duplessis, G.], *Petite Encyclopedie des Proverbes Français*. Paris, 1852.

Loubens, D., *Les Proverbes de la langue française*. Paris, 1889.

Mariette, A., *French and English Proverbs*. 3 vols. London, 1896–7.

Mésangère, P. de la, *Dictionnaire des proverbes français*. Paris, 1821.

Meurier, G., *Recueil de Sentences notables, dicts et dictons communs, proverbes et refrains.* Anvers, 1568.

Nucerin, J. A., *Proverbia Gallicana.* N.D. [1558].

Oudin, A., *Curiosités Françoises . . . avec une infinité de proverbes.* Paris, 1640.

Oursy, A. d', *Primer of French Proverbs.* London, 1883.

Pancoucke, J., *Dictionnaire des proverbes françois et des façons de parler comiques, burlesque et familieres, etc.* par P. J. P. D. L. N. D. L. E. F. Paris, 1749.

Payen-Payne, J. B., de V.,'*French Idioms and Proverbs* (Nutt). 1900.

Proverbes (Les Illustres) Novveavx et Historiqves expliqvez par diverses Questiones Curievses et Morales en forme de Dialogue divisez en devx Tomes avec une Suite non encore mise en lumiere. 1665.

Quitard, P. M., *Études Historiques et Morales sur les Proverbes Français.* Paris, 1860.

Quitard, P. M., *Dictionnaire Étymologique . . . des proverbes et des locutions proverbiales.* Paris, 1842.

—— *Proverbes sur les femmes, l'amitié, etc.* Paris, 1861.

Robertson, T., *Dictionnaire idéologique ; recueil des mots, des phrases, des proverbes, etc., de la langue française.* Paris, 1859.

Tuet, J. C. F., *Matinées Sénonoises ou Proverbes François.* Paris, 1789.

Wodroephe, John, *The Spared Hovres of a Soldier in his Travels. Or The True Marrowe of the French Tongue, with Sentences Proverbiales.* 1623.

Special.

Ballet des Proverbes, dansé par le Roi (Louis XIV.). 1654.

Montluc, A. de, *Comédie des Proverbes.* 1654.

Corblet, J., *Glossaire du Patois Picard (Proverbes, maxims et dictons Picards, ch. vi.).* 1851.

Crapelet, G. A., *Remarques . . . sur quelques locutions, proverbes et dictons populaires inédits du Moyen âge.* Paris, 1831.

De Jardin, J., *Dictionnaire des spots on proverbes wallons*

precèdé d'une étude sur les proverbes par J. Stecher.
Liège, 1891.

La Tour-Keyrié, A. M. de, *Recueil de Proverbes provençaux.* Aix. 1882.

Lespy, V., *Dictons et Proverbes du Béarn.* Pau. 1892.

Mattei, A., *Proverbes, locutions et maxims de la Corse.* Paris, 1867.

Noyons, A. J. D., *Proverbes et dictons àpropos des cloches.* 1884.

Pilot-Dethorey, J. J. A., *Proverbes dauphinois.* Grenoble, 1884.

Pluquet, F., *Contes Populaires préjugés, proverbes, etc., de Bayeux.* Rouen, 1834.

Proverbes et dictons agricoles de France. Paris, 1872.

Rolland, E., *Faune Populaire de la France, proverbes, etc.* 6 vols. Paris, 1879–83.

Toubin, C., *De quelques coutumes proverbes et locutions du pays de Salin (Jura).*

Sébillot, P., *Les poissons, proverbes dictons, etc., de Mer.* 1901.

ITALY,

Alfani, A., *Proverbi.* Torino, 1882.

Ambra, F. d', *Proverbi Italiani.* Firenze, 1886.

Cornazano, A., *Proverbii in facetie.* Paris, 1812.

Fabritii (A. C. degli), *Libri della origine delli volgari Proverbi.* Vinegia, 1526.

Finamore, G., *Vocabolario dell' uso Abruzzese.* (*Proverbi raccolti*, pp. 243–262). Lanciano, 1880.

Florio, J., *Il Giardino di Ricreatione (Ital. Proverbs).* 1591.

—— J., *Merie Proverbes, Wittie Sentences and Golden Sayings,* 1578.

Giusti, G., *Raccolta di Proverbi Toscani.* Firenze, 1884.

Lorenzo (da Volturino), *La Scienza Pratica. Dizionario di Proverbi.* Quaracchi, 1894.

Luri di Vassano, P., *Saggio di modi di dire proverbiali e di motti popolari Italiani.* Roma, 1872.

Mitelli, G. M., *Proverbi figurati.* Bologna, 1678.

Monosinii, A., *Floris italicæ linguæ libri novem.* Venetiis, 1604.

Morosi, G., *Studi sui dialetti greci della terra d'Otranto con una raccolta di Proverbi, etc.* Cecce, 1870.

Pasqualigo, Christofora, *Raccolta di Proverbi Veneti.* 3 vols. 1857–8.

Pavanello, M., *Proberbi, riboboli e detti proverbiali.* Vicenza, 1794.

Pirrone, F., *Raccolta di proverbi Tedeschi e Italiani.* Palermo, 1889.

Pitré, G., *Raccolta di Proverbi Siciliani.*

Poggiali, C., *Proverbi.* Codogno, 1881.

Polesi, G., *Dictionnaire des idiotismes italiens-français et français-italiens, proverbes, etc.* 2 vols. Boulogne, 1829.

Proverbii del Savio Romano dicto Schiavo de Barri, (printed at the beginning of the Sixteenth Century).

Strafforello, G., *La Sapienza del Mondo.* 3 tom. Torino, 1883.

Torriano, Giovanni, *Piazza Universale di Proverbi Italiani.* London, 1666.

——— *Select Italian Proverbs.* Cambridge, 1649.

"Tuscan Proverbs," *Fraser's Magazine.* Jan., 1857.

Varini, Julius, *Scuolo del Vulgo.* 1642.

SPAIN.

Adages et Proverbes Français extraits de Refranes o Proverbios del Comendador H. Nuñez (1555) in Génin, F. Récreations Philologiques. Tom. ii. p. 233–252. 1858.

Barros, A. di, *Proverbios Morales.* Madrid, 1598.

Burke, U. R., *Sancho Panza's Proverbs.* 1872.

——— *Spanish Salt, Proverbs in Don Quixote.* 1877.

B. y M., D. I., *Paremiologia, o tratado expositivo de los apotegmas proverbiales.* Valladolid, 1889.

Collins, J., *Dictionary of Spanish Proverbs,* compiled from the best Authorities, and trans. into English.

Haller, J., *Altspanische Sprichwörten und Sprich-wörtliche Redensarten aus den Zeiten vor Cervantes, in's Deutsche übersetzt in Spanischer und Deutscher Sprache erörtert, und verglichen mit den Entsprechen der alten Griechen und Romer, der Lateiner der späteren Zeiten, der sammtlichen Germanischen und Romanis-chen Völker.* 2 vols. Regensburg, 1883. With Bibliography of Books of Proverbs.

Nuñez, H., *Refranes Glossados.* Salamanca, 1578. (4 vols. Madrid, 1804.)

Oudin, C., *Refranes o Proverbios Castellanos.* Paris, 1608.

Sbarbi, J. M., *Monografia sobre los refranes, adagios y proverbios castellanos.* Madrid, 1819.

Yriarte, Juan, *Spanish Proverbs.* (MS. ?)

MISCELLANEOUS EUROPEAN

Adalberg, S., *Liber proverbiorum polonicorum.* Var-saviæ, 1889–94.

Ahlqvist, *Valittuja sananlaskuja Muorisolle* (Finnish proverbs for the use of the young). Helsingfors, 1896.

Baudartius, G., *Apophthegmata christiana, ofte gedenck-weerdige, leersame ende aerdighe spreucken van vele ende verscheydene christelicke persoonen.* Amst. 1640.

Čelokovský, F. L., *Mudroslovi národu slavanského ve přčalovich.* Praze, 1891–93.

Dahl, V., *Poslovitsui russkago naroda.* Moscow, 1862. (Proverbs of the Russian People).

Doyenhart, A., *Proverbes Basques.* Bayonne, 1892.

Düringsfeld, I. von., und Reinsberg, D. von, *Die Sprich-wörter der germanisch. und romanisch. Sprachen.* 2 vols. Leipzig, 1872–1875.

Gottlieb, I. L., *Fraseologi ; Danske Sætninger Mund-held, og Ordsprog.* Kjöbenh, 1882.

Gottlund, *De Proverbiis Fennicis.* Upsala, 1818.

Kristensen, E. T., *Danske Ordsprog og Mundheld.* Kjöbenh., 1890.

Lönnrot, E., *Suomen Kansan Sananlaskuja* (Proverbs of the Finnish People). Helsingfors, 1842.

Masson, M., *Mudrost narodnaya*. St. Petersburg, 1868 (The wisdom of the people in the proverbs of the Germans, Russians, French, etc.)

Oihenart, A., *Proverbes Basques*. Paris, 1657.

Voltoire, *Anciens Proverbes basques et gascons*. Paris, 1845.

Garay, E. de, *Maximes basques*. 1852.

Francisque-Michel, *Le Pays Basque*, pp. 29–42. Paris, 1857.

Poestion, J. C., *Lappländische Märchen, Volkssagen, und Sprichwörter*. Wien, 1886.

Proverbes Basques-Espagnols. Genève, 1896.

Safn af Islenzkum Ordhekvidhum. 2 vols. (Icelandic Proverbs). 1830.

Snegiref, J., *Ruskie v svoikh poslovitsakh*. 4 vols. Moscow, 1831–34. (The Russians in their Proverbs.)

Venizelos, K. J., *Collection of Neo-Hellenic Proverbs*. Athens, 1846.

Aravantinos, P., *Modern Greek Proverbs*. Janina, 1863.

Kigallas, I. de, *Collection of Modern Greek Proverbs*, in *Pandora*, vol. iii.

Constantinides, M., *Neohellenica*, pp. 245–248. London, 1892.

Vigfusson, G., and Powell, E. Y., *Icelandic Prose Reader*, 1879. (*Proverbs*, pp. 259–264.)

Záturecký, A. P., *Slovenská přslovi*. Praze, 1896.

CLASSICAL

Adagia quæcumque ad hanc diem exierunt, Pauli Manutii studio, cum indicibus græcis et latinis. Folio. Florentiae, Apud Juntas, 1575.

Adagia, id est, proverbiorum, paræmiarum et parabolarum omnium quæ apud Græcos, Latinos, Hebræos, Arabes, etc. in usu fuerunt, collectio. (*Erasmus, Junius, Alexander, Ulpius, Polydorus Vergilius, etc.*) Folio. Typis Wechelianis, 1629.

Binder, W. C., *Novus Thesaurus Adagiorum Latinorum.* Stuttgart, 1856.

Binder, W. C., *Medulla Proverbiorum Latinorum.* Stuttgart, 1856.

Del Rio, M., *Adagialia sacra Veteris et Novi Testamenti.* 2 vols. Lyons, 1614–18.

Erasmus, D., *Adagiorum Chiliades tres.* Venetiis, 1508.

Gaisford, T., *Parœmiographi Grœci.* Oxford, 1836.

Gartner, A., *Proverbialia Dicteria.* Erfurt, 1570.

Grüter, *Florilegium Ethico-Politicum.*

King, W. F. H., *Classical and Foreign Proverbs.* London, 1887. New edition, 1904.

Opsimathes, G. H., ΓΝΩΜΑΙ *sive Thesaurus sententiarum et Apophthegmatum ex scriptoribus grœcis prœcipue poetis.* Lips., 1884.

Otto, A., *Die Sprichwörter der Römer.* Leipzig, 1890.

Quarterly Review, " Greek Proverbs." July, 1868.

Sartori, J., *Adagiorum Chiliades Tres, sive Sententiœ Proverbiales Grœce, Latinœ et Belgicœ ex Prœcipuis Autoribus collectœ.* Amstelodami, 1670.

Schottus, A., *Parœmiographi Grœci.* Antwerp, 1612.

Thompson, D'A. W., *Sales Attici, Maxims of Athenian Tragic Drama.* Edinburgh, 1867.

Walker, W., *Parœmiologia Anglo-Latina.* 1676.

Zell, *Proverbs of the Ancient Romans (Ferienschriften,* ii. 1–96).

ORIENTAL, ETC

Agullini, T., *Proverbii utili e Virtuosi in lingua Araba, Persiana, e Turca gran parti in Versi.* Padova, 1688.

Ahmad Midhat, *Osmanli Proverbs* with English translations by E. J. Davis. London, 1898.

Bayan, G., *Armenian Proverbs and Sayings.* Venice, 1889.

Burckhardt, J. L., *Manners and Customs of the Modern Egyptians, illustrated from their proverbial sayings.*

—— *Arabic Proverbs of the Modern Egyptians.* 1830.

Burton, R. F., *Wit and Wisdom from West Africa.* 1865.

Burton, R. F., *Proverbia Communia Syriaca, in Journal of Royal Asiatic Soc.,* 1871, pp. 338–366.

Carr, M. W., *Collection of Telugu Proverbs, together with some Sanscrit Proverbs.* Madras, 1868.

Chhanu Lala Gupta, *Bunch of Eng. Proverbs, with equivalents in Urdu, Hindi, and Persian.* Delhi, 1892.

Chinassi, *Turkish Proverbs.* Constantinople, 1864.

Christian, J., *Behar Proverbs classified and arranged according to their Subject-matter,* with Translation and Notes, Appendix and Two Indexes, 1891.

Clergyman's Magazine, Nov. 1880. "A collection of Bengali Proverbs."

Davis, E. T., *Osmanli Proverbs and Quaint Sayings.*

Davis, J. F., *The Chinese.* (*Proverbs,* vol. ii., pp. 235–240). 1845.

Dennys, N. B., *Folk-lore of China,* 1876. See pp. 151–156.

Lister, "*Chinese Proverbs and their Lessons,*" in *China Review,* vol. iii. p. 129 *seq.*

Doolittle, J., *Social Life of the Chinese.* 1868. (*Chinese Proverbs,* pp. 534–537.)

Dukes, L., *Rabbinische Blumenlese, . . Talmudischer Sprichwörter.* Leipzig, 1844.

Fallon, W., *Dictionary of Hindustani Proverbs.* Benares, 1886.

Freytag, *Amsal el Arab.*

Galland, A., *Les Paroles remarquables . . . et les Maximes des Orientaux.* La Haye, 1694.

Gray, J., *Proverbs from Burmese Sources.* London, 1886.

Gurdon, P. R., *Some Assamese Proverbs.*

Jellinek, A., *Der Jüdische Stamm in nicht-jüdischen Sprichwörten.* Wien, 1886.

Jensen, H., *A Collection of Tamil Proverbs.* London, 1897.

Johnson, W. F., *Hindi Proverbs with English Translations.* Allahabad, 1898.

Knowles, J. H., *Dictionary of Kashmiri Proverbs,* Bombay, 1885.

Koelle, S. W., *African Native literature, proverbs, etc.,
in the Kanuri or Bornu language.* 1854.

Landberg, C., *Proverbes du People Arabe.* Leide, 1883.

Lazarus, J., *Dictionary of Tamil Proverbs.* Madras,
1894.

Long, J., *The Proverbs of Eastern Nations.*

———— *Oriental Proverbs and their uses,* in *Trans. of
Oriental Congress,* 1874, pp. 380–395.

Manwaring, A., *Marathi Proverbs* (W. India). 1899.

Mawr, E. B., *Proverbele Românilor.* London, 1882.

Morris, J., *English Proverbs with Hindustani parallels.*
Lahore, 1898.

Oihenart, A., *Proverbes basques avec des poésies basques.*
Bordeaux, 1847.

Percival, P., *Tamil Proverbs, with their English translations.* Madras, 1874.

Perny, *Proverbes Chinois.* Paris, 1869.

*Prabodhaprakasa Sena Gupta ; Dictionary of Proverbs,
Bengali and English.* Calcutta, 1899.

Ragusa-Moleti, G., *I Proverbi dei popoli barbari,*
Palermo, 1893.

Rhasis, D., *Collection de Proverbes en Arabe, Persan, et
Turc.* Constantinople, 1889.

Rochiram Gajumal, *Handbook of Sindhi Proverbs.*
Karachi, 1895.

Scaliger, I., et Erpenii, T., *Proverbiorum Arabicorum
Centuriæ duæ cum Interp. Latina et Scholiis.* Lugd.
Bat., 1623.

Scarborough, W. A., *Collection of Chinese Proverbs
translated.* Shanghai, 1875.

Shortland, E., *Traditions of the New Zealanders* (*Proverbs,* pp. 196–201), 1856.

Smith, A. H., *Proverbs of the Chinese.* Shanghai, 1888.

Tallquist, K. L., *Arabische Sprichwörter und Spiele.*
Helsingfors, 1897.

Taylor, W. E., *African Aphorisms ; or Saws from Swahili
Land translated and annotated.* London, 1891.

Tendlau, A., *Sprichwoerter u. Redensarten deutsch-
jüdischer Vorzeit.* Frankf. 1860.

Tennent, J. E., *Christianity in Ceylon* (*Singhalese Proverbs,* pp. 346–348). 1850.

" *The Shade of the Balkans,*" *A Collection of Bulgarian Proverbs.* 1904.

Thorburn, *Pushtoo Proverbs.*

Wazir Ahmad, *English Proverbs with Urdu equivalents.* Bareilly, 1892.

Butler & Tanner, The Selwood Printing Works, Frome, and London